Audit Risk and
Audit Evidence

Audit Risk and Audit Evidence:

The Bayesian Approach to Statistical Auditing

Anthony Steele
Ernst & Young Professor
Warwick Business School
University of Warwick
Coventry, UK

ACADEMIC PRESS
Harcourt Brace Jovanovich, Publishers
London   San Diego   New York
Boston   Sydney   Tokyo   Toronto

ACADEMIC PRESS LIMITED
24–28 Oval Road
London NW1 7DX

US edition published by
ACADEMIC PRESS INC
San Diego, CA 92101

A catalogue record for this book is available from the British Library

ISBN 0-12-664140-4

Typeset by Photo·graphics, Honiton, Devon
Printed and bound in Great Britain at Mackays of Chatham PLC,
Chatham, Kent

Contents

Acknowledgements

This research was supported by the Technical and Research Committee of the Chartered Association of Certified Accountants (ACCA). The ACCA supports research as a contribution to discussion, and for the advancement of accounting knowledge, but does not necessarily share the views expressed, which remain the sole responsibility of the author. Nevertheless, I would particularly like to thank Roger Adams of the ACCA and Michael Mumford of Lancaster University for their contributions to the preparation of this study. Naturally, I remain responsible for errors and omissions.

Preface

This book is concerned with coherent and defensible judgement in an audit context. The text has its origins in a short series of lectures delivered at the University of Lancaster 1984–85. The objective was to popularize and make accessible to third-year undergraduates some of the latest research, almost wholly US in origin, into formal models for quantifying and evaluating uncertainty. The presentation was mathematical at an intermediate level, presuming that students had followed a basic course in probability and statistics for business studies or foundation accounting. The aim of the course was to provide a blend of theory and application, studying problems of both practical relevance and theoretical interest, selecting key papers for exposition.

The course, it must be confessed, was not an outstanding success, not entirely due to the indolence of the students. (The expedient of blaming the victims is always a well rehearsed device for instructors.) One difficulty was that there was no suitable text. Another problem was the appropriate balance between rigour and detail on the one hand and breadth and appreciation on the other. Too much (any?) maths puts people off. This book reflects further thoughts on these compromises and the intention to reduce the mathematics to its simplest. The basic message of this book draws only on simple Bayesian results.

Education, we are told, is what remains when we have forgotten the details. When the details are forgotten then the argument made here is that prior judgement can be quantified by being considered as equivalent to already having taken and tested a sample of audit evidence. Quantification is merely the process of making explicit what is implicit. The decision support tools to implement this approach already exist as prototypes. Advances in micro-computing imply that the costs of implementing a formal quantified approach have plummeted, altering quite radically previous evaluations of the costs and benefits. Whether the balance has altered sufficiently for the approach I describe to be adopted by the profession is for the future to tell.

ANTHONY STEELE

Chapter 1

A Service to Risk Sharing

1.1 Introduction

For every £20 of all business done in the UK, whether it is from consumers shopping in the High Street to businesses buying from their suppliers, somewhere between 1 and 2 pence goes to audit firms.[1] Auditing is conducted on a very large scale. Not only does the activity consume financial resources, in recent years the audit firms have recruited a large proportion of UK graduates irrespective of their subject area. It represents the modal first employment destination for the graduate workforce. Nearly one in six graduates going into employment in 1987 opted for an accountancy training course. Peat Marwick McLintock that year recruited more than 1000 graduates—almost as many as the UK's entire intake into social work.[2] The large audit partnerships are international operations with the top eight each having a world fee income well in excess of £500 million (in 1988). This is a significant economic activity. But what is its significance? What is the economic role of auditing? What functions does the audit serve? What are the sources of demand for this service?

The simple answer is we do not know for sure. However, we do have interesting hypotheses. Some of our explanations are surprising in that they are not the way that accountants have traditionally understood their business—the risk business.

There are two classes of stories told about the economic role of auditing. For convenience these are labelled here as: (i) the information hypothesis, and (ii) agency theory.

1.2 The information hypothesis

The information hypothesis is that shareholders demand audited financial information about companies because financial information is needed to determine market values, which in turn are the means of making rational investment decisions. It is believed that investors demand audited financial statements because they provide information that is useful in their investment decisions.

If the audit industry was pressed for an economic justification, then it would probably turn to the idea of adding value to financial information. Lee[3] from a review of the literature picks out a particular passage as typical:

> ... The following statement would appear to express the current conventional wisdom of auditing:

> ... no one would deny that the function of the auditor, in lending credibility to financial statements, has been growing in importance, rapidly and steadily over the last fifty years ... Such financial reports are relied on heavily by investors, creditors, security analysts, Government and others. The role of the auditor, in lending credibility to these financial statements, is vital in establishing and maintaining confidence in the capital markets. Without such confidence the whole basis of our capitalist system would be destroyed. Thus, the continuing importance of the auditors role is not in dispute.[4]

The story is that certification services are valuable because financial statements are relied on heavily by users. There are several anomalies to this rationale. The discordant evidence which undermines this explanation comes from studies of how the financial markets actually work, and from surveys of the information needs of users.

Work on how financial markets behave[5] has established that they do not just react very quickly to information. Financial markets anticipate news. Daily price changes are random. This random movement is because prices only change in response to any unanticipated information.[6] There is a large number of analysts and other information intermediaries looking to see if they can anticipate price movements using the information in the series of past prices (the weak information set), or in publicly available information (the semi-strong information set), or in, dare one say, insider and non-publicly available information (the strong information set). The result of this activity is that investors are making use of a broad range of information networks and sources, most of it unaudited, rather than relying merely on published accounts. Furthermore, the speed of information release is crucial to its value. Ball and Brown,[7] in a pathbreaking study of the speed of reaction of price changes to the release of annual audited accounts, found that most of the price change due to the formal announcement had occurred at least a month before the announcement occurred. They concluded:

> However, the annual income number does not rate highly as a timely medium, since most of its content (about 85 to 90 percent) is captured by more prompt media which perhaps include interim reports. Since the efficiency of the capital markets is largely determined by the adequacy of its data sources, we do not find it disconcerting that the market turned to other sources which can be acted upon more promptly than annual net income.

Foster[8] in a study of interim earnings announcements (unaudited) found that these have substantially more information content than annual audited earnings announcements by a factor of about 3.[9] This finding that investors rely on a wide variety of information sources, most of it unaudited but all of it timely, tends to conflict with the assertions of the information hypothesis. Indeed, given the importance of timeliness of information, one could make a case that, because auditors delay the earnings announcement, they therefore reduce the value of the information rather than add to it! For example, Fanning[10] estimated that the average delay for listed UK companies between the year-end and the publication of the annual report was over 100 days. This delay he largely attributed to the audit process.

The second class of discordant evidence about the informational importance of audited accounts is the small number of studies on the information needs of investors. These indicate that investors rely in the main on sources which are unaudited, such as Chairmen's statements, or press reports. Commenting on this area, Lee says:

> Baker and Haslem (1973), in an analysis of 851 individual investors, found that of the three factors rated by their respondents as 'of great importance', two were related to the future economic outlook of the company and its industry. Of the next seven most important items, four related specifically to the future. If information were to be provided to satisfy these needs, it would presumably have to be of a predictive nature and, therefore, not subject to the type of audit scrutiny and opinion given to historic data. In support of this, Baker and Haslem further found that 62% of their respondents rated stockbrokers and other advisory services as the most important information sources, with a further 11% rating the financial press as the primary source. Only 8% similarly rated financial statements which, in their annual format, would be audited. None of these findings lends much credence to the assumed importance of the audit function in the use of financial information, although audited data may be used indirectly in many of the unaudited sources.[11,12]

In the light of such research, we must conclude that the link between certification services and value added to the information for decision making is more tenuous than conventional wisdom allows.

1.3 Agency theory

The information hypothesis sees auditing as a service to investors and other users who demanded information. An alternative and complementary explanation sees auditing as a service to risk sharing.

Company law and institutional capital markets in Britain both allow the institutional devices of limited liability, together with security classes with differing rights, including a residual class of investors that is prohibited from sharing in a firm's wealth until an income threshold has been passed. Companies are managed by a technocracy which might have no equity stake in the firm but has control over the wealth and information flow. In such an environment there is considerable scope for conflicts of interest. In its simplest form the honesty and integrity of the company directors as stewards of the assets entrusted to them by the owners is an issue. In some circumstances this conflict can be resolved by nepotism. Appointing managers only from amongst members of one's family is a device that works in small-scale enterprises, particularly in less developed economies. Another device is using a caste system which extends the pool of talent that an economy can draw on for its managerial class. The social sanction is disgrace, 'black-balling', ostracism and exclusion. Vestigial remnants of such arrangements survive to this day in the UK. For instance, until only recently the insurance market at Lloyds operated its syndicates without members (the names) having to receive audited accounts. The previous control system with its emphasis on honour and exclusivity of membership could be characterized as a caste system. As an economy develops one can see how auditing evolves as a more effective arrangement, widening the pool of talent from which managers can be drawn. Resolving simple shareholder–manager conflict of interest, auditing can be seen as a service to the managerial labour market. In recent years theorists have come to recognize that the demand for a monitoring service does not derive exclusively from shareholders but also comes from managers. Shareholders can allow for the scope and discretion of managers to deviate from their interests by reducing compensation contracts. To avoid this managers have an incentive to bind themselves to limiting their own scope for adverse action by engaging auditors. The argument is illustrated by the diagram given in Figure 1.1.

With early primitive social control mechanisms the demand curve for managers is reduced because of agency costs from c_1 to c_3. As managers are a factor of production, an economy operating at this level must restrict the scale of its investments and its activity. By evolving a more efficient control device, such as auditing, some of the agency costs are mitigated and the demand for managers and also their wages rise from c_3 to c_2. The economy then operates at a higher level of investment since the risks of doing business are reduced. Whilst this is an interesting story, one could not take the auditor's contribution to wealth creation too far since international evidence suggests that advanced capitalist economies can function equally well with alternative arrangements and without large-scale auditing activity.[13]

Another source of conflict of interest and hence demand for auditing is between debt holders and equity holders. A conse-

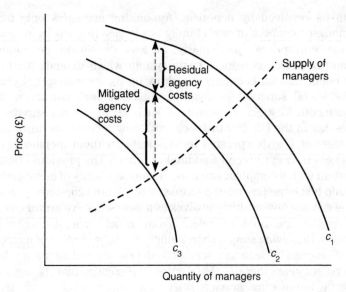

Figure 1.1. A service to the managerial labour market. c_1, Economy demand for the managerial factor of production in the absence of agency costs; c_2, economy demand for managers with agency costs mitigated by auditing; c_3, economy demand for the managerial factor of production with agency costs with nepotism and caste but in the absence of auditing.

quence of limited liability is that shareholders can choose to undertake riskier projects than debt holders might like. This is more easily seen with a numerical illustration.

Example 1.1

Suppose a firm has to choose between two risky projects, A or B. The present value of these investments depends on the state of the economy. For simplicity there are only two states, boom or slump, and they are considered to be equally probable (see Table 1.1). It is evident that project A could be thought better than project B. It has, on average, a greater present value, and it has less risk because it performs pretty much equally well under boom or slump.

Now let us consider how the project looks if the enterprise has 100 worth of loans to repay (see Table 1.2). In this case

Table 1.1. The pay-offs for each state of the economy for the projects A and B of Example 1.1.

	State of economy		
	Boom	Slump	Average
Project A	110	100	105
Project B	160	−100	3

Table 1.2. The pay-offs for each state of the economy when projects A and B of Example 1.1 have 100 worth of loans to repay.

	State of economy		
	Boom	Slump	Average
Project A	110−100=10	100−100=0	5
Project B	160−100=60	−100−100=0*	30

* Due to limited liability: zero is the result of subtracting a 100 loan repayment from a negative present worth of 100.

project B dominates project A since they both give the same return in a slump—but project B gives six times the pay-off of project A in boom times. This simple example demonstrates that in the presence of limited liability shareholders can benefit at debt-holders' expense by choosing risky projects. For equity holders the protection of limited liability means that losses and gains do not have to be equally balanced. Debt holders by contrast would prefer project A, since they only participate in the down-side risk. If a business does well their up-side gain is limited to the settlement of the nominal amount of the debt, but if a business suffers they can share the pain. Such conflicts of interest between classes of capital give rise to complex covenants, debentures and contractual arrangements concerned with managing risk. These agreements need policing, monitoring and auditing. Thus auditing is a service to risk sharing through resolving conflicts of interests between classes of money capital.

Recent arguments[14] more directly offer a justification of the economic role of auditing in terms of providing insurance in the event of financial loss from business failure. Again a simple numerical illustration is in order.

Example 1.2

Imagine an entrepreneur who is planning a new venture which offers the following pay-offs: $+2000$ if it is a success, and -1000 if it is a failure. It does not matter that the chance of failure is small, and that everyone involved with the project will be working hard to avoid such a catastrophe. This size of risk might be considered unacceptable. The venture is too much of a lottery for anyone to take it on. However, now suppose that for a fixed fee of 500 someone would agree to cover the losses in the event of failure, then the situation would be as shown in Table 1.3. The effect of the insurance agreement is that the original risk $(+2000, -1000)$ has been split in two $(+1500, -500)$ and $(+500, -500)$. These smaller scale risks might now be acceptable both to the entrepreneur and to the auditor. There has been risk sharing. As Wallace[14] expresses it:

> Auditors have 'deep pockets' relative to a bankrupt or ailing corporation that cannot pay. Based on courts' inclinations, auditors can provide protection from an otherwise uninsurable business risk of investment. The courts have tended to assume that the auditor is the guarantor of the accuracy of financial statements to consumers (investors) who are deserving of protection from

Table 1.3. The situation in Example 1.2 if losses in the event of failure are covered for a fee of 500.

	Entrepreneur's position before insurance	Entrepreneur's position after insurance	Insurer's position
Success	2000	2000−500 fee = 1500	+500 fee
Failure	−1000	0–500 fee = −500	−1000 payout + 500 fee = −500

financial loss. The courts appear to view the auditor as a means
of socializing risk. In other words, because he is held responsible
for business failures, the auditor in turn shifts this cost to clients
through higher fees and then to society through higher prices and
lower returns on investment.

In this account auditing is conceived as part of the risk-sharing
process in which large unbearable risks become smaller bearable
ones.

As an explanation for the demand for auditing this insurance
hypothesis has been given some weight in the US courts. In the
case Rusch Factors vs Levin (1968) the Court asked:

> Why should an innocent reliant party be forced to carry the
> weighty burden of an accountant's professional malpractice? Isn't
> the risk of loss more easily distributed and fairly spread by
> imposing it on the accounting profession which can pass the cost
> of insuring the risk onto its customers, who can in turn pass the
> cost onto the consuming public?

This is quite a radical view of the economic function of auditing,
particularly at a time when the UK profession is worried about:
(i) the burden of unlimited liability; (ii) being jointly and severally
liable (the greater the number of partners, the greater the risk!);
and (iii) the rising cost of professional indemnity insurance.

If auditors were to see themselves as insurers they might:
change the basis of charging so that risk was taken into account;
refuse to offer certification services to certain high-risk industries;
require clients' employees to have fidelity bonding insurance as
a pre-condition of accepting assignments; insist that directors in
client companies and other officers had their own professional
indemnity insurance so that there were more 'deep pockets'
around; develop a range of certification levels, e.g. fully comprehensive, or no payroll defalcations in excess of £20 000; and so
on.

It is not yet the case in the UK that the courts have seen the
auditor as insurer. On the contrary, in the Irish Woollen Co vs
Tyson (1900) case the court described the duties of the auditor
in the following terms:

> He is not an insurer against fraud or error; and if fraud is alleged
> it must be shown with precision the acts of negligence for which
> he is said to be responsible.

However, here is not the place to comment on the legal

position. In describing the information hypothesis, theory was
contrasted with the empirical evidence. So far, in telling some
of the stories that go under the generic title of agency
theory, some of the empirical evidence which supports these
interpretations of the economic role of auditing has been avoided.

1.4 Some empirical evidence

Agency theory has now become the dominant framework for
researchers trying to understand, explain and predict accounting
phenomena. From this body of work, the prize winning study by
Chow[15] is particularly supportive of the present discussion. Chee
Chow looked at the situation in the US in 1926, a period before
there were compulsory audit requirements. Although there were
no legal requirements in place to obscure the workings of a free
market, auditing was performed. Chow formulated the following
hypotheses to predict the sorts of circumstances in which auditors
would be engaged voluntarily:

H_1 *ceteris paribus*, the smaller is the manager's ownership share
in the firm, the higher is the probability that the firm
voluntarily engages external auditing.

H_2 *ceteris paribus*, the higher the proportion of debt in a firm's
capital structure, the higher is the probability that the firm
voluntarily engages external auditing.

H_3 *ceteris paribus*, the greater the number of different accounting
numbers in a firm's debt covenants, the higher is the
probability that the firm voluntarily engages external auditing.

H_4 *ceteris paribus*, the larger a firm's total size, the higher is
the probability that it voluntarily engages external auditing.

Before considering the extent to which these predictions are
borne out, one should note the connection of these hypotheses
with the theory or simple stories that have been described. The
attraction of agency theory is that it does produce testable
predictions. The hypotheses are really conditional predictions,
i.e. *if* other things are held equal *then* these events can be
expected to occur. The problem with predictions in the non-

experimental sciences is that one cannot control the conditions as well as in a laboratory, and so there can be difficulties in repeating or replicating a study because of the shortage of data.

Chow found 65 over the counter (OTC) companies and 379 New York Stock Exchange (NYSE) listed companies on 31 December 1926 for which data were available. He chose all the OTC and 100 of the NYSE companies. For each company in the sample, four variables were measured:

Firm size (SIZE) = market value of owner's equity + book value of debt

Debt/equity ratio (DE) = book value of debt/SIZE

COVNUM = the total number of different accounting measures used in all of its debt instruments

MGRSHR = A proxy for the percentage of common stock (or 'ordinary shares') owned by officers and directors of the company. The proxy was used because this information for each company was not available; instead only industry aggregated data were available.

The basic results of the study are set out in Table 1.4. The summary statistics listed in the table indicate that companies which chose voluntarily to engage auditors were:

(i) on average larger than those that did not (whether the average is measured by the middlemost point (median) or by dividing the sum by the sample number (mean)), H_4;

(ii) on average had more borrowing, H_2;

(iii) on average had more accounting based covenants written into their loan contracts, H_3; and

(iv) on average were in industries with larger managerial ownership in the firm. This is contrary to the prediction of hypothesis H_1.

This is such an elegant piece of accounting research that it is not over-indulgence to quote directly from its summary and conclusions:

This study uses an agency theory framework to analyze firms' incentives to hire external auditing. It postulates that a major

Table 1.4. The basic results of the study by Chow:[15] medians, means and standard deviations (SD) of the independent variables.

		Entire sample		NYSE sample		OTC sample	
		Audited (N = 110)	Not audited (N = 55)	Audited (N = 79)	Not audited (N = 21)	Audited (N = 31)	Not audited (N = 34)
SIZE (× 10⁶)	Median	$13.80	$9.23	$27.77	$24.75	$6.52	$4.72
	Mean	$54.27	$26.35	$73.06	$49.69	$11.94	$6.37
	SD	($143.2)	($44.86)	($165.5)	($64.3)	($14.9)	($6.95)
DE	Median	0.008	0.000	0.036	0.001	0.002	0.000
	Mean	0.136	0.064	0.139	0.059	0.128	0.067
	SD	(0.190)	(0.120)	(0.188)	(0.101)	(0.196)	(0.131)
COVNUM	Median	1.237	0.675	1.25	0.375	1.208	0.885
	Mean	1.518	0.909	1.481	0.524	1.613	1.147
	SD	(1.332)	(1.093)	(1.30)	(0.68)	(1.430)	(1.234)
MGRSHR	Median	22.69%	17.45%	22.70%	11.43%	22.62%	17.83%
	Mean	25.92%	19.87%	26.12%	15.03%	25.42%	22.86%
	SD	(15.29%)	(14.74%)	(15.49%)	(13.07%)	(14.97%)	(15.1%)

reason for firms to hire this service is to help control the conflict of interests among firm managers, shareholders, and bondholders. Firm characteristics which affect the severity of this conflict or the marginal cost of external auditing are expected to influence a firm's demand for this service. Based on this analysis, leverage, firm size, and number of accounting-based debt covenants are predicted to increase the probability that a firm will voluntarily hire external auditing. The firm manager's ownership share is predicted to have the opposite effect.

Data on the selected firm characteristics were collected for 165 NYSE and OTC firms for 1926. Both univariate and multivariate tests were performed. The results generally supported the hypothesized effects of leverage and accounting-based debt covenants. There was some support for the importance of firm size. Measurement problems precluded an adequate test on manager ownership share.

Overall, these results suggest that agency cost considerations play an important role in the external auditing decision. The existence of such private incentives may imply a reduced need for auditing regulations.

1.5 Audit regulation

Professional accountants might recoil with horror at the thought of removing the requirement in the Companies Act for all companies to have an audit. In a political climate in which de-regulation and privatization are in vogue, the prospect is not unthinkable. Politicians are more aware of the phenomenon of 'regulatory capture' in which, although the vocabulary justifying regulation is in terms of the protection and benefit of the general public, the industry which is being regulated finds that the rules operate to its own advantage. As far as the auditing industry is concerned, the Companies Act: (i) requires all companies to purchase the service of auditors; and (ii) provides a barrier to entry to the industry by restricting the classes of persons who can offer the service of auditor.

Regulatory capture is one type of regulatory failure. The term 'regulatory failure'[16] is used to describe the situation in which the consequences of laws are worse than the market failures that they seek to remedy. This occurs because laws, regulations, accounting standards and so on have a habit of growing in both number and complexity as time passes. Whilst regulations are frequently elaborated and added to, they are seldom simplified or revoked. The burden of compliance is often unrecognized by regulators, who in any event are lobbied by experts who may have a vested interest in the *status quo*. There is a scenario in which a radical pro-free-enterprise administration, in order to remove the burden on business, removes the legal requirement for audit. If the predictions of agency theory are correct, there would still be a large demand for audits. Any fall in demand would come from low-geared small businesses and from closely owned and managed companies. It is in just such enterprises where conducting an audit is difficult. Rather than being a disaster, de-regulating auditing might, paradoxically, bestow benefits on auditors. As far as this monograph is concerned, deregulating audit certification would make the present discussion even more pertinent as the industry comes to view itself less as a legal service and more explicitly as a market service, and a service to risk sharing.

Notes and references

1   See, for example: M.E. Haskins and D.D. Williams (1988) The association between client factors and audit fees: a comparison by country and by firm, *Accounting and Business Research*, **18** 183–190.

2   R. Waters (1989) The race is on to replace a rare commodity, *Financial Times*, (11 May 1989) 13.

3   T.A. Lee (1977) The modern audit function: a study of radical change. In: B. Carsberg and T. Hope (Eds). *Current Issues in Accounting*, pp. 87–106. London: Philip Allan.

4   E. Stamp and C. Marley (1970) *Accounting Principles and the City Code: The Case for Reform*, pp. 168–169. London: Butterworth.

5   This is an extensive modern literature on this area. For a readable account see R.L. Watts and J.L. Zimmerman (1986) *Positive Accounting Theory*. USA: Prentice-Hall International.

6   See P.A. Samuelson (1965) Proof that properly anticipated prices fluctuate randomly, *Industrial Management Review*, **6** 41–49.

7   R. Ball and P. Brown (1968) An empirical evaluation of accounting income numbers, *Journal of Accounting Research*, **Autumn**, 159–178.

8   G. Foster (1977) Quarterly accounting data: time series properties and predictive-ability results, *The Accounting Review*, **Jan.**, 1–21.

9   For a discussion of this issue see Watts and Zimmerman, pp. 49 ff. (see note 5).

10 D. Fanning (1978) How slow are the auditors in Britain? *Accountancy*, **Aug.**, pp. 44–48.

11 Lee (see note 3).

12 H.K. Baker and J.A. Haslem (1973) Information needs of individual investors, *Journal of Accountancy*, **Nov.**, 64–69.

13 E. Stamp and M. Moonitz (1979) *International Auditing Standards*. London: Prentice-Hall.

14 W.A. Wallace (1980) *The Economic Role of the Audit in Free and Regulated Markets*. New York: Touche Ross.

15 C.W. Chow (1982) The demand for external auditing: size, debt and ownership influences, *The Accounting Review*, **Apr.**, 272–291.

16 A. Belkaoui (1985) *Accounting Theory*, pp. 48 ff. Orlando: Harcourt Brace Jovanovich.

Chapter 2

Managing Risk

2.1 Introduction

When one talks to a medical practitioner about professional risk, one is quickly made aware that there can be undesirable consequences for a doctor to dwell on this aspect of health care. The phrase 'defensive medicine' was coined to describe the debilitating condition in which a doctor is motivated to avoid a bad decision rather than make a good one. For its doctors, society does not want professional self-protection placed before all other considerations. At times, serious chances need to be taken by intelligent individuals with coolness and resoluteness. As a patient one hopes that medical risks do not over the course of time come to mean risks to medics!

By contrast, the professional judgement of an auditor should concentrate on himself. In offering certification services the accountant assumes legal responsibilities and voluntarily participates in risk. Unlike the doctor, whose legal exposure is incidental to his principal service, the auditor's legal exposure is at the crux of his service. The whole activity of gathering audit evidence can be characterized from the auditor's perspective as a process of managing risk. The letter of engagement which sets the bounds of the work, all the procedures of quality control, the detailed programme of work and the formula and disclaimers chosen for the final report are all activities whose purpose is to manage risk. It was discussed in Chapter 1 that a major explanation of auditing is as a service to risk sharing. It follows that risk management goes to the core of the audit process. The auditor is not concerned with minimizing risks, because the least risk is to refuse to certify, or to certify while disclaiming any responsibility for the opinion. A senior partner once quipped 'an opinion is the free-est thing in the world. Everyone will have an opinion. The trick is to sell it ...'. What makes an opinion something one sells, rather than something one gives away, are the risks and liabilities that are taken on with it. The auditor, in providing opinions, is intimately concerned with managing risk and with balancing risks.

From the work of Otway and Pahner[1] there are four stages in controlling and managing risks. These stages seem to be broadly applicable to a variety of contexts such as geophysical hazards (floods, hurricanes, earthquakes, etc.), biological hazards (epidemics, food contamination, health care, etc.), technological hazards (civil engineering, the nuclear industry and chemical manufacture), geopolitical hazards (war, insurrection and terrorism) or financial hazards. The four stages of risk management are as follows.

(i) Risk identification and classification—what are the sources of danger?
(ii) Risk estimation—how big are the dangers?
(iii) Risk evaluation—can we live with the dangers?
(iv) Risk prevention—can we take action to mitigate the consequences of unfortunate events?

Most of the attention of formal audit teaching as reflected in major textbooks and in professional syllabuses is largely concerned with the first and last stage of the risk management process. Teaching is concerned with such factors as: how to identify potential weaknesses in accounting control systems; what are the principles of sound internal control; what methods of investigation are available; what are the characteristics and types of evidence; and how to design and conduct a comprehensive

testing programme. The last stage of the risk management process
dealing with the forms of words for audit reporting, the phrasing
of letters of comfort, professional ethics in handling conflicts of
interest, independence, handling fraudulent clients, business
failures, and so on, also receive attention. In this chapter the
primary concern is the neglected middle two stages of the
process, i.e. how to form a view on the acceptability of risks.

   Until recently, not just in auditing but also in many fields,
professional judgement was considered to be a topic beyond
enquiry. Unlike legal judgements, professional judgements are
frequently protected from scrutiny by the requirements of
confidentiality. Expertise was only derived from experience. It
was a domain of knowledge that could not be articulated, it could
only be communicated by observation. Judgement constituted a
secret knowledge handed on in unconscious ways from master
to disciple. Whilst elements of such gnosticism will remain
important, recent years have witnessed a flowering of interest
from researchers in many fields on the processes of judgement,
in knowledge engineering, and in designing expert systems. Whilst
audit judgement has been neglected in the textbooks, it has not
been neglected in the research journals. Before becoming
immersed in the detail of this work, some general observations
on these four stages are appropriate.

2.2 Risk identification

As stated above, in selling certification services the accountant
must take on legal responsibilities. The value of the service
derives from the responsibilities which are taken on. These
responsibilities can crystallize into liabilities under certain
circumstances. As has been stated, the precise conditions and
grounds for the liabilities to crystallize are well recounted in the
leading textbooks and so are not covered here. In general terms
the textbooks analyse the reasoning processes behind legal
decisions in order to offer guidelines to predict the decisions of
courts. However, identifying the auditor's potential sources of
risk is only the first step of the risk management process. Indeed,
there are two limitations of the conventional jurisprudential
approach should the first step remain the only step: (i) the

frequency and incidence, and hence importance, of various circumstances are not quantified; and (ii) particularly in the UK, most cases are settled before they come to court, so that relevant case law on which to predict the decisions of courts is quite sparse.

There has been very little empirical study of the historical frequency of legal risks to auditors. There has only been one study of the reasons for cases brought against accountants and this was on US cases. This work by St Pierre and Anderson[2] starts with the simple question, 'What gets public accountants into trouble with clients and third parties?' To answer the question St Pierre and Anderson did an enormous amount of work in tracking down 129 cases in the USA where one of the defendants was an accountant or auditor. The exercise was difficult because legal indexing of cases is by points of law, rather than by specific type of defendant. They then analysed the reason for or cause of the dispute. Auditing was only involved in 65% of the cases involving accountants (taxation and other services accounted for the rest). Interesting findings which they report were as follows.

(i)   Errors in the execution of audit engagement were in the minority. Only 28% of cases were considered to be about audit procedures; the majority of claims were concerned with inadequate disclosures (e.g. omission of information on significant losses, or omission of significant liabilities) or disputes about accounting treatments (e.g. asset valuation, revenue recognition, capitalizing vs expensing transactions, and consolidation transactions).

(ii) Client fraud was involved in 12% of cases, and fraud by the auditor in 7% of cases.

(iii) Bankruptcy, significant client losses and investigations subsequent to merger were the most frequent triggers for legal action.

(iv) Certain industries were over-represented as a source of trouble. Companies in the service sector were less involved than might be expected, but finance, insurance, property and manufacturing companies, accounting for only 15% of US companies, were involved in 46% of the cases.

(v)   Not a single case was concerned with excessive conserva-
       tism. No suit concerned undervaluing assets, recognizing
       excessive expenses or inadequate amounts of revenue.

The value of this type of research is that, if the findings could
be generalized, an auditor could direct resources to the important
areas of:

(i)   shifting resources out of detailed procedural checks into
        focusing professional judgement on disclosure issues
        and contentious accounting policy choices;
(ii)   predicting high-risk engagements using bankruptcy and
        merger prediction models;
(iii) avoiding high-risk industries, or charging premium rates
        for involvement; and
(iv)   erring on the side of conservatism.

One could contrast this approach with the conventional mode
of research in large accounting firms which is known as 'red
flagging', i.e. drawing attention to an individual case. Some firms
circulate a 'fraud of the month' in their technical bulletins to
staff. Interesting as such single instances are, they do not help
resource allocation in audit planning. On the contrary, the danger
with red flagging is that attention is directed to the rare but well
publicized case, and away from the more likely but mundane
and un-newsworthy causes of trouble.

The study by St Pierre and Anderson was conducted on US
cases but, as noted earlier, UK disputes are usually settled
without reaching court. In order to get data on the incidence
and frequency of disputes, one would have to analyse indemnity
insurance claims. Despite the current importance of the whole
indemnity insurance issue to the accounting profession both in
the UK and in North America, there has been surprisingly little
research published on this topic. Schultz and Gustavson[3] tried
to investigate the judgements of those responsible for setting the
premiums for professional liability insurance in the USA. They
found that only six insurers in the USA were writing insurance,
and that 'virtually all of the "Big Eight" firms acquired their
insurance through Lloyd's of London'. Being US academics, they
were unable to extend their study to the UK. Their questionnaire
survey obtained only five usable responses and established little.
In an intriguing study of negligence claims in the UK, Woolf[4]

made some limited analyses of the experience of a scheme arranged by one of the Accounting Institutes for its members, through Bowrings. Large accounting firms seek cover on an individual basis, so the scheme covers only the majority of small practitioners. Table 2.1 shows a classification of claims.

In the more recent period 1973–82, auditing was responsible for only 22% of the claims by number, but 40% by value. Reliance by third parties on negligently certified accounts comprised 3.2% of claims (5.82% by value), and failing to detect defalcations amounted to 6.25% of claims (14.56% by value). Interesting as these data are, one should bear in mind that the experience of

Table 2.1. Analysis of negligence claims—a 10-year survey.[*]

Area of professional work	Number of notified claims (% of total)		Monetary amount claims (% of total)	
	1966–75	1973–82	1966–75	1973–82
Auditing				
Failing to detect defalcations	13.71	6.25	14.32	14.56
Reliance by third parties on negligently audited accounts	7.53	3.20	6.34	5.82
All other audit work	8.91	12.60	59.26	19.72
Taxation				
Late elections—general	13.01	8.33	4.24	8.71
Failure to claim stock relief	NA	2.75	NA	3.58
All other tax work	18.49	29.50	2.18	14.40
Liquidation/receivership work	4.79	3.35	0.26	1.22
Executorship/trusteeship work	3.42	3.75	0.77	3.50
Negligence investment/financial advice	8.90	4.70	3.92	4.40
Fraud and dishonesty of partners and employees	7.53	2.61 1.53		14.64
Libel, slander/loss of documents		3.16		0.43
All other claims—unspecified	13.71	19.80	7.08	9.02

NA, not available.
[*] From Woolf.[4]

small firms of accountants is likely to be quite different from the large firms in the industry. Furthermore, the domain of Woolf's study[4] was broad, on the general area of the legal liability of accountants, rather than focused on analysing the particular risks of auditors.

This actuarial/statistical approach to analysing disputes in terms of causes has been a neglected approach in identifying risks. Professional research in risk identification has thus far been dominated by studying the points of law involved and 'red flagging'.

2.3   Risk estimation

Once risks have been categorized the next step is to decide how large they are. Estimating risks requires data collection, evidence gathering and empirical observation. This raises several questions. How much should be collected? What is adequate evidence? How does one derive estimates from data in a defensible way? These questions go to the core of the audit process and the formation of a defensible opinion. Subsequent chapters look at what is involved in the quantification of estimates and at the research on ways to make such judgements explicit.

2.4   Risk evaluation

Making evaluations involves forming judgements about whether risks are acceptable, that is to say, whether they are greater or less than some acceptable criterion. One can seldom afford the costs associated with zero risks, so that trade-offs are involved. How does one decide whether a risk is acceptable or not? What are the components of an auditor's decision? As with risk estimation, these are the major neglected questions which are discussed in the chapters that follow.

2.5 Risk prevention

Fischhoff *et al.*[5] advocate three strategies for handling risks:

(i) prevention of events that trigger unfortunate consequences;
(ii) prevention of consequences once events have taken place; and
(iii) mitigation of consequences once these have occurred.

A most attractive strategy must be to avoid or prevent the trigger events. For example, when driving a car, one does not speed, abuse alcohol, or drive recklessly; one avoids accidents. However, accidents happen. Wearing a seat belt would be strategy two. It would prevent some of the consequences in the event of an accident. Carrying motor insurance, health-care insurance, loss-of-earnings insurance might be an example of strategy three, mitigating the consequences once an accident has occurred. For the auditor, prevention of the events that trigger unfortunate consequences is also an attractive strategy. Quality control is the generic term used to describe steps taken under this strategy. Quality control embraces a litany of procedures:

(i) developing and sustaining a business culture and organisational ethos that places a high value on professional integrity and reputation;
(ii) selecting, training and motivating staff;
(iii) developing standardized procedures, documentation and manuals in accordance with best practice; and
(iv) using peer and second partner reviews and so on.

Weinstein[6] has described an extension to conventional quality control used in the US firm of Touche Ross & Co. which is formally designed to reduce trigger events. The firm assesses risk on each of its clients using a check-list similar to that given in the Appendix to this chapter, advocated by Bertschinger.[7] He writes:

At the completion of the process we expect to:
- Have identified all of our significant risks and possibly achieved an early warning system to potential problem situations.
- Better match our partner and staff resources against the high risk situations.

- Adopt strategies to minimize risk either through increased audit coverage, through the use of industry expertise, or through different forms of reporting and disclosure.
- In appropriate instances, we will use this information to eliminate risk situation from our practice.

The assessment of risk is intended to be an annual event which we believe can substantially improve the quality of our practice.

However, an enormous amount of quality control would be needed to prevent every accident. The second and third general strategies for handling risk are concerned with damage reduction. In the specific audit context, a defensible opinion is the major component of a strategy concerned with reducing damage. In the following chapter I turn to the detail of defensible audit opinions.

Notes and references

1   H.J. Otway and P.D. Pahner (1976) Risk assessment, *Futures*, **8** (2).
2   K. St Pierre and J.A. Anderson (1984) An analysis of factors associated with lawsuits against public accountants, *Accounting Review*, **Apr.**, 242–263.
3   J.J. Schultz and S.G. Gustavson (1978) Actuaries' perceptions of variables affecting the independent auditor's legal liability, *Accounting Review*, **Jul.**, 626–641.
4   E. Woolf (1985) *Legal Liability and Practising Accountants*. London: Butterworth.
5   B. Fischhoff, C. Hohenemser, R. Kasperson and R. Kates (1980) Handling hazards. In: J. Dowie and P. Leferere (Eds). *Risk and Chance*, pp. 161–179. Milton Keynes: The Open University Press.
6   E.A. Weinstein (1986) International commentator, *Proceedings of 4th Jerusalem Conference on Accountancy, Audit Risks and the Increasing Burden of Unlimited Liability*. Institute of Certified Public Accountants, Israel, p. 153.
7   P. Bertschinger (1986) Switzerland national paper, *Proceedings of 4th Jerusalem Conference on Accountancy, Audit Risks and the Increasing Burden of Unlimited Liability*. Institute of Certified Public Accountants, Israel, pp. 93–97.

APPENDIX 2:1
Audit risk check-list—conditions indicating the possible existence of increased risk

An analysis of risk is an important element of management's responsibilities and is perhaps an aspect of management that is not at present adequately recognized. The auditor cannot assume this responsibility, but must be aware of those conditions which may indicate increased risk when planning the audit. Examples of such conditions are given below.

I. Line of business
    (1) Strong competition.
    (2) Rapid change, such as a high technology industry.
    (3) A declining industry characterized by a large number of business failures.
    (4) Nationalization.
    (5) Legal constraints (e.g. on expansion, on production etc.) for political, environmental or other reasons.

II. Geographical area
    (1) Political unrest.
    (2) Large sales or other company activities in countries or areas where questionable activities are known to be common or boycott rules are applied.
    (3) Inadequate transport facilities.

III. Staff, organization and business procedures
    (1) Highly domineering senior management and/or an ineffective board of directors/audit committee.
    (2) Indications of management override of significant internal controls.
    (3) Compensations of significant share options tied to reported performance or to a specific transaction over which senior management has actual or implied control.
    (4) Indications of personal financial difficulties of senior management.

(5) Significant litigation, especially between shareholders and management.

(6) Excessively optimistic earnings forecasts.

(7) A complex corporate structure where the complexity does not appear to be warranted by the company's operations or size.

(8) Widely dispersed business locations accompanied by highly decentralized management.

(9) Understaffing which appears to require certain employees to work excessive hours or to cancel holidays.

(10) High turnover rate in key financial positions such as financial director or controller.

(11) Frequent change of auditors or lawyers.

(12) Known material weaknesses in internal controls which it is practicable to correct but which remain uncorrected.

(13) Illegal acts or other violations of company policy which are not remedied.

(14) Material transactions with related parties or transactions that may involve conflicts of interest.

(15) Unusual(ly) large payments in relation to services provided in the ordinary course of business to lawyers, consultants, agents and others (including employees) (i.e. conditions which indicate the use of intermediaries for large or unusual transactions).

(16) Difficulty in obtaining audit evidence with respect to:
    (i)   unusual or unexplained entries;
    (ii) incomplete or missing documentation and/or authorisation; or
    (iii) alterations in documentation or accounts.

(17) Unforeseen audit problems, for instance:
    (i)   client pressures to complete audit in an unusually short time or under difficult conditions;
    (ii) sudden delays; or
    (iii) evasive or unrealistic responses of management to audit inquiries.

(18) Recent disclosure by other companies in the industry of illegal or questionable acts.

(19) The existence of large negotiated sales to foreign governments.

(20) Dealing through agents or other intermediaries on bases different from those normally followed with customers.

(21) Selling prices or commissions for foreign sales unusually in excess of those for domestic sales.

(22) Offers of rebates to customers other than in the customer's country of residence.

(23) Evidence of non-operating subsidiaries, secret bank accounts, or other hidden funds.

(24) Risk of strikes and blockades.

IV. Earnings and operating budgets

(1) Decline in the volume or quality of sales (e.g. increased credit risk, sales at or below cost, and lower profit margins).

(2) Significant changes in business practices.

(3) Dependence on a single or relatively few products, customers, or transactions for the continuing success of the business.

(4) Lack of product development.

(5) Excess capacity.

(6) Unrealistic production targets.

(7) Slow replacement and reduced depreciation of production plant.

(8) Significant fluctuations disclosed by analytical review procedures which cannot be reasonably explained, for example:
  (i) unusual accounts balances in relation to nature of account;
  (ii) unusual physical inventory variances; or
  (iii) unusual inventory turnover rates.

(9) Large or unusual transactions, particularly at year-end, with a material effect on earnings.

V. Assets

(1) Decrease in asset values.

    (2)   Inadequate physical security with risk of interruption of operations.

VI.   Liquidity and financing
    (1)   Inadequate cash flow.
    (2)   Insufficient working capital.
    (3)   Lack of flexibility in borrowing requirements such as working capital ratios and limitations on additional borrowings.
    (4)   Lack of equity capital.
    (5)   Difficulties in obtaining new equity capital (for instance due to ownership, regulatory or legislative provisions).

VII.   Unexpected losses
    Arising from unfavourable developments affecting:
    (1)   Purchase and sales contracts.
    (2)   Subcontract agreements.
    (3)   Contracts of guarantee.
    (4)   Product warranties.
    (5)   Leasing contracts.
    (6)   Foreign exchange positions.
    (7)   Insurance coverage.

Chapter 3

Coherent Audit Judgements

3.1 Introduction

Although there is some debate over the nature of the economic service offered, the blunt fact is that auditors are employed to express an opinion on whether accounts prepared by management are fairly stated. Auditors are liable for their judgements and require evidence to support them. The auditors' liability for their opinions is an incentive mechanism which has the tendency to make them encourage management to state accounts fairly. There are, of course, countervailing influences at work in the preparation of accounts. These influences derive both from the (in)adequacy of the systems of internal control to be self-checking and also from the exercise of managerial (in)discretion. Managers can have incentives to influence auditors. The auditor's judgement involves negotiating and weighing up the countervailing influences. Fortunately auditors are not liable in law to certify accounts as accurate,[1] but only as 'true and fair'. This weaker criterion allows for some tolerance away from 100% accuracy in accounts. This tolerance is reflected in paragraph 4 of the UK Auditing Standard, 'the auditor's operational standard' which states that:

> The auditor should obtain relevant and reliable audit evidence sufficient to enable him to draw reasonable conclusions therefrom.

The Auditing Guideline, 'audit evidence' expands on this:

> The auditor can rarely be certain of the validity of the financial statements. However, he needs to obtain sufficient relevant and reliable evidence to form a reasonable basis for his opinion thereon. The auditor's judgement as to what constitutes relevant and reliable audit evidence is influenced by such factors as:
>
> (a) his knowledge of the business of the enterprise and the industry in which it operates;
> (b) the degree of risk of misstatement through errors or irregularities; this risk may be affected by such factors as:
> (i) the nature and materiality of the items in the financial statements;
> (ii) the auditor's experience as to the reliability of the management and staff of the enterprise and of its records;
> (iii) the financial position of the enterprise;
> (iv) possible management bias;
> (c) the persuasiveness of the evidence.

What the guideline does not say is how one judges the sufficiency of evidence. How should a reasonable man evaluate evidence, incorporate it into his judgement and decide on its adequacy? In estimating risks how much data should be collected? How does one derive estimates from data in a defensible way? In evaluating risks how does one decide whether or not a risk is acceptable?

It is to such questions we now turn. Before proceeding it is necessary to make the following comments. We are not concerned with the situation in which there is no ambiguity about the conclusions to be drawn from evidence, for example when an auditor tests an entire set of data (100% testing), or obtains authenticated certification direct from a third party, e.g. a confirmation of an account balance direct from a banker. Our questions are only challenging in the context of audit sampling, where an auditor seeks '... to draw conclusions about the entire set of data ("the population") by testing a representative sample of items selected from it ...' (paragraph 4 of *Exposure Draft*

Auditing Guideline on Audit Sampling). The second observation is that the ultimate test for the auditor is not how a reasonable man makes a judgement, but how the courts make a judgement. This distinction is made because the arguments which I advance here have never been tested before the English Courts. In a review of these issues McRae[2] observes that he '... could find no legal case anywhere which had attempted to define an adequate audit sample'. It is the prerogative of judges and juries to decide what is reasonable, and what are generally accepted standards. However, it was noted earlier that there are many other legally untested issues in auditing. The courts would be guided by expert witnesses (i.e. other auditors' views on the adequacy of audit performance) and by authoritative literature. On this point authoritative writing in the exposure draft on audit sampling exhorts in paragraph 5, 'The auditor should use a rational basis for planning, selecting and testing the sample and for evaluating the results so that he has adequate assurance that the sample is representative of the population, and that sampling risk is reduced to an acceptable level'.

The rational basis which I discuss here is concerned with formal quantified models of judgement. However, it should be stated from the outset that in discussing the rational basis for judgement one is unavoidably in the normative/didactic area of how judgements ought to be made (although I will later mention some of the positive research on how judgements are made). In the auditing literature this question of the quantification of judgement vs non-quantification is misleadingly referred to as the judgement vs statistical sampling issue.

3.2 Judgement versus statistical sampling

At its worst, judgement sampling can be little more than a euphemism for a totally haphazard examination of items without any judgement about the appropriate volume of testing other than 'the same number as last year', without any judgement about the sufficiency of evidence.

Survey evidence reported by McRae[3] indicates that in the UK the use of judgement sampling is overwhelming. Whilst a few of the world's largest accounting firms, particularly those having strong North American connections, make use of statistical sampling, only about one in ten medium sized firms claims to use statistical sampling in any form on any jobs. The authoritative professional literature also endorses the view that:

> A rational basis can be achieved using either non-statistical or statistical sampling, provided in either case it is properly carried out ....

Despite this evidence that the non-quantified approach is required as a generally accepted auditing standard, it must be considered inadequate on a number of grounds.

(i) Judgement sampling uses evidence in ways which are not articulated in clear logical steps, so that there is no basis for understanding the processes involved.

(ii) Without clear understanding of how evidence and judgement are linked, it is not possible to improve judgements or to change procedures. One is locked into the *status quo*, and has no basis either for adapting to change or for defending audit decision, for example in court in response to an action.

(iii) Since judgement sampling lacks any formal notion of improvability, or optimality in the amount of evidence collected or how it is interpreted, it must inevitably lead to a misdirection of resources—some areas will be over-audited, and other areas under-audited. Although one might suspect it, one will not have the grounds to know if this is happening.

(iv) Judgement sampling provides no conceptual framework for teaching and communicating risk judgements. In large firms these are important needs.

By contrast, formally quantifying judgements offers the following advantages.

(i) A formal framework allows one to understand the processes involved, to study judgement, and to clarify thinking. From understanding it is possible to adapt to change.

(ii) Quantification can improve risk judgements by providing stronger evidential support, since evidence is evaluated in a logically defensible way.

(iii) A formal framework makes training and education easier. It also assists in the communication of judgements.

(iv) Using formally quantified judgements can reveal surprises and insights which are not obvious and may conflict with intuition and everyday common sense.

In the face of such a list of disadvantages of one approach and benefits of the other approach, it is natural to wonder why the former persists as the dominant form in practice. There are three answers to this. The first is that the quantification of judgement requires investment in training and investment in computing so that there is a difference in set-up costs. In an industry with a rapid labour turnover, an approach which might lead to long-term cost savings may not be in the short-term interest of any firm. For any one firm to invest heavily in technical innovations presents the risk that staff will leave and take the knowledge with them, so competitive advantage will be lost to firms who have not paid the costs.

The second explanation which can be advanced is 'The law of the flat bottom'. This law is the bane of management science and relates to the fact that very few business decisions are knife-edged, and one can move quite a distance from the best decision and still make a good one. So businessmen can make adequate stock ordering decisions without knowing the results of the economic analysis of optimal order quantities, they make sensible capital budgeting decisions without understanding net present values, they make not bad travelling salesmen without knowing shortest route algorithms (other than end the day near home, then it is not so far to drive!). Figure 3.1 shows how this law might apply in the audit evidence context.

The curve OAB plotted in Figure 3.1 shows the increase in value for increasing the amount of evidence. The curve has a decreasing gradient since there are diminishing marginal returns to increases in evidence. In the limit increasing evidence drives away all uncertainty and one has perfect information. The line FC shows the costs of evidence. For simplicity of exposition, there are no changing returns to scale, but a simple fixed (F) and variable cost structure. Evidence is collected because its value exceeds its cost. At a certain point A, the marginal value of additional evidence is less than its marginal cost, so the point

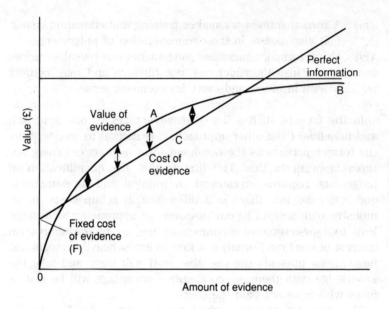

Figure 3.1. Audit evidence and the law of the flat bottom.

is reached where an optimal amount of evidence is collected. The gain from sampling is the difference between its value and its cost (AC).

Figure 3.2 shows this gain from sampling, which is equivalent to the curve OAB minus the line FC in Figure 3.1. This figure

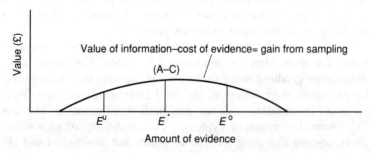

Figure 3.2. Audit evidence and the law of the flat bottom. E^*, optimal amount of evidence; E^u, too little evidence (under-auditing); E^o, too much evidence (over-auditing).

clearly shows that there is an optimal amount of evidence marked (E^*) which could, in a quantified decision context, be calculated.[4] Although there is a maximum point the curve in Figure 3.2 is very flat so that, whilst over-auditing (E^o) or under-auditing (E^u) are sub-optimal, they might not represent too costly a loss of efficiency when, for example, employing low cost labour on unimportant jobs. There is a small irony, of course, in that one can only offer this explanation of the preponderance of the non-quantitative approach to sampling from the theoretical framework of a quantitative approach!

The third reason for the persistence of judgement sampling is that, until recently, the application of management science in this area was limited by the lack of computing available to field auditors. Lacking the interactive computing needed to analyse small samples, the statistics advocated for auditors relied on large numbers. The result was that, added to the obscure language in which the results of classical statistics are stated, uneconomic sample sizes were recommended.

Now, with advances in micro-computing technology, and the use of portable and lap-top computers by field auditors, more applicable quantitative methods are available. The choice between quantifying and not quantifying judgement is becoming less clear-cut. All the commentators see the future as bringing decision support tools in auditing using expert systems concepts. These concepts are based on formal quantified models of judgement. Whilst this is in the future it is the author's belief that auditors need to study formal models of judgement in order that they understand the informal models which underlie contemporary practice, and can answer the questions about the sufficiency of evidence and the defensibility of judgement posed earlier.

3.3 Quantifying judgement

Is 'quite probable' less certain than 'more likely'? Is 'fairly certain' more probable than 'most possible'? English is rich with phrases for describing uncertainty in judgements, but the phrases do not have any generally accepted and agreed meaning. Moore and Thomas[5] have reported some evidence of this.

These authors looked at the ranking of uncertainty expressions

Table 3.1.   Ranking of uncertainty expressions.*

Expression	Average rank	Range of ranks
Quite certain	1.10	1–3
Expected	2.95	1–4
Likely	3.85	2–7
Probable	4.25	2–9
Not unreasonable that	4.65	3–7
Possible	6.10	3–9
Hoped	7.15	3–10
Not certain	7.80	3–10
Doubtful	8.60	7–10
Unlikely	8.75	3–10

* From Moore and Thomas.[5]

taken from a literary style article on forecasts in the consumer durable field. Some 250 managers attending courses at the London Business School were asked to rank 10 various expressions in order of the decreasing certainty that they implied. The results of this exercise are presented in Table 3.1.

Commenting on these results Moore and Thomas[5] stated that:

> The final column shows the range of ranks given to each of the 10 expressions, illustrating ... the inconsistency between the respondents. Indeed, only one set of four of the 250 taking part produced precisely the same rankings. In a further experiment ... the results showed that respondents were not even consistent over time.

Breadth of vocabulary and swapping the changes with synonyms is fine for a refreshing literary style, but has limitations in communicating risk judgements. One needs a more precise language for graduations of judgement. The Committee on Basic Auditing Concepts of the American Accounting Association (1969–71) in playing with synonyms state:

> ... these varying degrees of assurance ... refers to these varying degrees of conviction as degrees of credibility—the probability that a given assertion is true or valid ....

It is to probability theory we turn for quantifying judgement. Now for most of us, probability is not associated with judgement. It is something to do with tossing coins or drawing cards. It has a 'true' objective value. This objective interpretation of probability has a legitimate philosophical grounding. Objectivists view probability as a fundamental property of nature (like mass, conductivity, distance or other physical quantities). It is supposed to 'exist' and have some determined 'true' value. Estimates of 'true' objective probability are made by considerations of symmetry, where identical experiments repeated under identical conditions should have the same 'true' probability of success. Thus observation of frequencies in the limit give the 'true' probability of an event. This objective concept of probability is one that is particularly appropriate in the experimental sciences, and is the notion of classical statistics, which is about the asymptotic results of repeated sampling. So that when one says 'the probability of a head is a half', it can be considered as shorthand for 'if a fair coin was repeatedly tossed, then in the limit the frequency of heads would equal the frequency of tails'. Such a concept of probability has nothing to do with judgement, it is a statement of experimental fact. When such a concept of probability is applied in auditing then it leads to statements such as: 'If samples of this size were repeatedly drawn from this population, and an interval of confidence calculated in a certain way, then the frequency with which such intervals would straddle the true but unknown mean of the population, would in the limit equal 95%'. Such a statement is a statement of fact about the results of an auditor repeatedly conducting an experiment, repeatedly taking a particular sample and calculating an interval or range in a certain way. It is not a statement about judgement.

Auditing is about judgement. Objective probability, despite its impeccable credentials and its roots in experimental science, is not the vehicle required here. An alternative view, and, I shall argue, a more useful one, is subjective probability.

3.4 Subjective probability

Bernouilli's 1713 treatise, *Ars Conjectandi* (*The Art of Guessing*) is credited with being the earliest source to define probability as the degree of confidence in a proposition the truth of which we cannot be certain. To a subjectivist, probability is simply a numerical score that is given to a statement to indicate a degree of confidence in it. A score of 100% is given if we are certain in our judgement that a statement is true, and we give a score of 0% if we are certain in our judgement that a statement is false. If we are unsure we give a score between 0% and 100%. So the statement 'this coin will land heads side up when it is tossed', might be given a score of 50%, because we are equally balanced in our judgement whether the statement is true or not. In shorthand we might still say 'the probability of a head is a half', but now we are making an expression of our subjective judgement, rather than a statement of objective 'in the long-run' fact.

At this stage the distinction may seem a bit philosophical and pedantic, but as we go on we see that subjective probability is a practical tool for understanding and describing audit risk judgements. Objective probability is about experimental facts. It does not make sense when it is used in contexts which are not experimental. For example, if we say: 'The probability that this accounting treatment complies with the accounting standard is 50%', then as a subjective probability statement it makes sense as a quantified judgement. However, one would have difficulty interpreting this statement as an objective probability statement. There are no long-run series of accounting treatments which when infinitely repeated converge in frequency of legality to a half. Subjective probability as a quantification of judgement is then clearly more applicable in the auditing context, since many judgements are about unrepeatable or non-experimental events.

3.5 Coherence

Subjective probability is the language of judgement. Its vocabulary is real numbers in the interval 0 to 1, or between 0% and 100%, but what of its grammar? It was noted above that statements which are certainly true take a score of 100%, and those of certain untruth take a score of 0%. How are the numbers in between used? Formally subjective is defined by the set of bets which a decision-maker is prepared to accept. De Finetti[6] comments:

> It is a question simply of making mathematically precise the trivial and obvious idea that the degree of probability attributed by an

individual to a given event is revealed by the conditions under which he would be disposed to bet on that event.

Just as an objectivist when thinking of probability must conceive of some experiment which has a long-term frequency limit, so an auditor in order to quantify judgement using subjective probability has to imagine allocating money to the alternatives. For example, suppose an auditor had to give a range estimate for an accounting error in which he was 50% confident, then he could imagine having to put half his money on the range and the other half outside the range. Say the range of error estimate is plus or minus £5000. Then, because the auditor is only 50% confident, he should be indifferent to betting in the range or outside of it (see Figure 3.3.). Again consider what a 90% judgement interval for the proportion of errors in attribute sampling might be. Most likely the auditor might consider that there were zero errors. For a 50% interval he might put half his money on the error proportion being less than 0.06, and 90% on this error being less than 0.14.

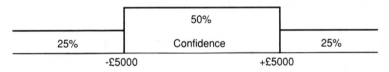

Figure 3.3. A 50% judgement estimate for the size of an error in an accounting population.

In Figure 3.4 the judgemental weight that is given to each proportion is represented by the area under the curve. So if the judgement is that there is only a 10% chance that the proportion of errors exceeds 0.14, then this is represented by a thin area under the judgement curve. The total area under the curve must be 100% otherwise the judgement is incoherent. To see this imagine that a judgement is expressed as follows (see Figure 3.5):

Event A: a 50% chance that the absolute value of the error is less than or equal to $100 000.
Event B: a 40% chance that the error is more than +$100 000.
Event C: a 30% chance that the error is less than $100 000.

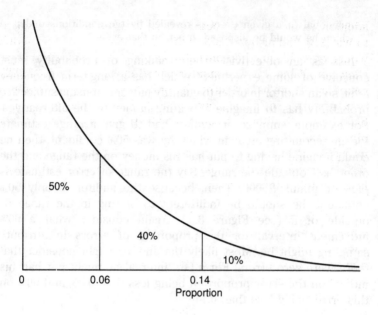

Figure 3.4. Judgements about a proportion.

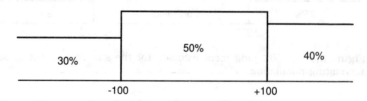

Figure 3.5. An incoherent judgement.

It is intuitively obvious that judgement weights cannot add up to more than 100%. Formally the incoherences are also obvious from the connection with book-making. Probability weights of $x\%$ correspond with odds of $x:100\text{-}x$ in a fair bet. So a 40% probability is a $2:3$ gamble. In offering the incoherent judgement weights of Figure 3.5, an auditor can be considered formally as being indifferent to fair bets on three mutually exclusive events. To demonstrate incoherence of judgement one could hypothetically require him to bet on all of them. For such an auditor to put £10 on event A in the hope of gaining £23.33 in addition would be a fair bet. So would putting £10 on event B to win £10, and also to bet £10 to win £15 on event C. The book would be made in the conventional turf-accounting manner as shown in Table 3.2. The auditor would stake in total £30 (£27 net of lay-off) to have returned in total at most £25 (£15 winnings + £10 stake) since only one event A, B or C can occur. The hypothetical auditor has had a hypothetical book made against him revealing his incoherent quantification of judgements. For mutually exclusive events we formally require that the sum of the judgement weights should equal 1 or 100%. Using conventional notation this can be written as

$$P(A) + P(B) + P(C) = 1$$

where $P(\cdot)$ is the probability or judgement weight. Arguments such as the one above can be advanced to show that our numerical measure for uncertainty obeys the usual laws or axioms of probability.[7]

For illustration one of the most fundamental of the rules for probability is the rule of additivity. This requires that the probability weight given to one or other of two contradictory propositions is the sum of their probabilities. Using an illustration from Shafer and Srivastava this can be explained as follows.[8]

Table 3.2. The conventional turf-accounting book for the example given in the text.

| | | Payout | | |
| | | Event C less than −100 000 | Event A ±100 000 | Event B more than +100 000 |
	Stake			
Bet No.				
1	10	−33.33		
2	10		−20	
3	10			−25
Subtotal	30	−33.33	−20	−25
Lay-off	−3	+10		
Total takings/ payouts	27	−13.33	−20	−25

The probability of a particular account receivable being collected within 60 days after a sale, for example, is equal to the probability of its being collected within 30 days plus the probability of its being collected between 30 and 60 days.

Let A and B denote two contradictory propositions, let C denote their disjunction, the proposition A or B.

The rule of additivity says

$$P(C) = P(A) + P(B)$$

Thus if A denotes collect within 30 days and $P(A) = 30\%$, and B denotes collect between 30 days and 60 days and $P(B) = 40\%$, then C denotes collect within 60 days and $P(C) = 30 + 40 = 70\%$.

If an auditor's judgement does not obey this rule, for example $P(C) > P(A) + P(B)$ then it is possible to make a book. The betting-rate interpretation for judgement says that the auditor is willing to take either side of a bet on A at odds $P(A):(100-P(A))$, either side of a bet on B at odds $P(B):(100-P(B))$, and either side of a bet on C at odds $P(C):(100-P(C))$. We offer to bet £$P(A)$ on A, £$P(B)$ on B, and £$(100-P(C))$ against C. The auditor must put up £$(100-P(A))$, £$(100-P(B))$ and £$P(C)$. There are three possible outcomes, and in each case the net gain is £$P(C)-P(A)-P(B)$.

(i)   A is true. In this case B is false and C is true. The gain from bet A is £$(100-P(A))$. The loss on bet B is £$P(B)$ and the loss on bet C is £$(100-P(C))$. The total winnings are:

£ $(100-P(A) - P(B) - (100-P(C)) = $ £$P(C) - P(A) - P(B)$

(ii) B is true. In this case A is false and C is true. The gain from bet B is £$(100-P(B))$. The loss on bet A is £$P(A)$ and that on bet C is £$(100-P(C))$. The total winnings are:

£$(100-P(B) - P(A) - (100-P(C)) = $ £ $P(C) - P(A)-P(B)$

(iii) A and B are both false, in this case C is also false. The gain from bet C is £$P(C)$ and the losses on bets A and B are £$P(A)$ and £$P(B)$, respectively. The total winnings are:

$$£P(C) - P(A) - P(B)$$

If, however, the auditor's judgement is $P(C) < P(A) + P(B)$, then by reversing all bets, the net gain is $£P(A) + P(B) - P(C)$, betting $(100 - P(A))$ against A, $£(100 - P(B))$ against B, and $£P(C)$ for C.

The intricacies of book-making, and the axioms of probability have volumes devoted to their exposition. It is sufficient here to state that, provided that it is coherent, subjective probability obeys all the logical relationships necessary for it to be used in a formal quantitative model of judgement. The proviso that probability is coherent restricts our models not to the actual working of auditors' minds (since actual auditors may be only more or less coherent in their judgements, just as real auditors may not actually reason according to the axioms of logic). The sting with the proviso is that reasoning which does not obey the rules of logic is illogical, and judgements which violate the rules of probability are not rational and must be considered to be less defensible.

3.6 A model of audit judgement

The discussion so far has been at a general level rather higher than the set of practical questions posed in the introduction to this chapter. However, without yet concerning ourselves with the problems of implementation we have established the idea that it might be possible to represent judgemental weight by the area under a curve. Before turning to how this can be done in practice, we will push this idea a little further and build a model of audit judgement. Thereafter, we will have a framework for discussing the details. The model is based on Steele[9] and consists of the following components:

p_i^* a set of single-point values for the elemental propositions from which the financial statements are constructed. These single-point values are the assertions of management to which the auditor is required to attest, such as the historic cost of fixed assets, the total value of invoices in a period and so on.

m_i a corresponding set of materiality intervals for each elemental proposition. The materiality interval gives the acceptable range of values which the auditor is prepared to accept. For example, for assertion 'cash at bankers = £1 million', or 'provision for obsolete stock = £0.3 million', quite different ranges of accuracy might be appropriate.

$f(p_i)$ is the set of subjective probability density functions where the area under each part of the curve represents the auditor's judgement of the variety of values that a particular proposition could take.

Consider, for example, a single proposition, auditing the sales ledger. Suppose management assert that receivables total £10 million, then $p_i^* = £10$ million. If the auditor decides that he should err on the side of conservatism he might decide that he will tolerate errors of £0.25 million if they are understatements, but only £0.10 million for errors of overstatement, so $m_i = (-0.25, +0.10)$. These quantities may be represented diagrammatically as shown in Figure 3.6, with the auditor's quantified judgement superimposed. The judgement weight is spread out reflecting the wide range of values that the auditor believes at this stage. The hatched area represents the auditor's probability or the weight

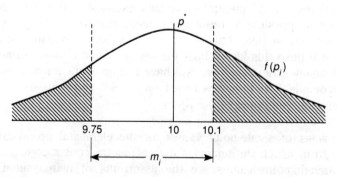

Figure 3.6.   Elements of the model.

of judgement that the asserted value $p^* = £10$ million is either over- or under-stated.

At the tactical planning stage of the audit, i.e. in deciding how much attention is to be given to each proposition and where to allocate resources, the auditor's decision could be modelled in these terms. Minimal effort might be directed to certain propositions because the probability beliefs fall inside the acceptable range, either because for some reason the auditor was prepared to accept a wide range of beliefs, or because the auditor felt less uncertain based on prior experience. Formulating a subjective probability density before collecting any evidence, but based on prior experience alone, is known as 'choosing a prior'. An auditor can have grounds for choosing a prior based on previous years work, experience on comparable jobs in comparable situations, discussions with and evaluation of the management, and using decision support tools which help in making the choice.

As the auditor learns more about the organization under audit by means of systems review, compliance testing and substantive testing, then the prior probabilities become revised (or posterior). The programme of audit testing on a proposition usually ceases once the auditor's judgement weight falls inside the acceptable range given by the materiality for that proposition.

Figure 3.7 shows the audit opinion as the result of comparing the posterior set of beliefs with the assertions (p_i^*) and the set of materiality intervals (m_i). It should be stressed that at this stage of describing the model I am glossing over the practical details of how the auditor incorporates evidence into his prior beliefs. This is, of course, not a mere detail since it concerns how evidence is used to substantiate opinions in a defensible way. Collecting evidence changes the weight of judgement attached to various values so that, hopefully, they become more concentrated. With complete knowledge the judgement weight condenses to a single point with 100% of the probability density at that point.

Figure 3.8 illustrates the process for the example of auditing a sales ledger. With complete knowledge the auditor is certain that the sales ledger is £9.95 million, shown by all the probability weight massed at this point. However, certainty is a costly state to arrive at, because it corresponds to 100% testing. Since the auditor is not required to certify accounts with 100% accuracy,

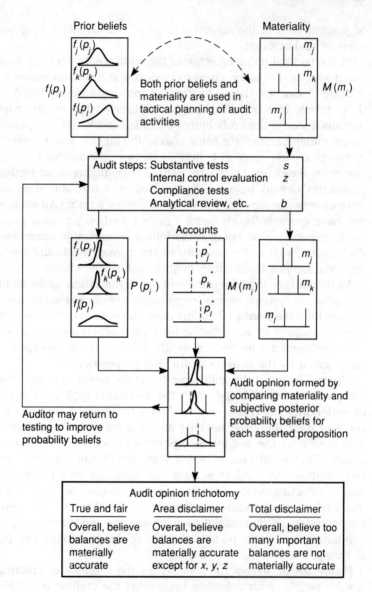

Figure 3.7. Model of audit opinion forming.

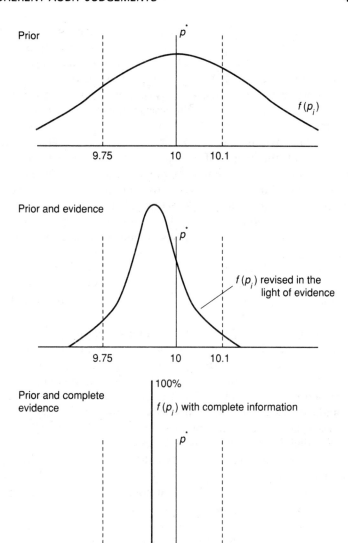

Figure 3.8. Revising judgement in the light of evidence.

testing can cease once the judgement weight is sufficiently massed. Again at this stage I must gloss over what constitutes sufficient massing as well as glossing over the exact process by which prior judgements become 'massed' by evidence.

In considering an individual proposition there are four cases which could arise. These are illustrated in Figure 3.9. In case (a), the auditor's subjective posterior probability distribution is substantially within the materiality range of the management's assertion of the value of the particular proposition, and the auditor's best point estimate of the value of the proposition is the same as management's asserted value, p_i^*. This case requires no special action. If all propositions are like this (or like case (b) below) the auditor gives a 'clean' audit report; his attestation lends credibility to the assertions of management. The tails of probability distributions that lie outside the materiality range give the auditor's perception of his risk of making an error. The costs of errors if they are subsequently revealed are largely borne by the auditor, since he attests to a proposition which is subsequently found to be materially in error. The auditor's overall perception of the risk that he buys in signing an audit report is a composite of the probability of errors for all propositions, with the probabilities that errors will subsequently be discovered, together with the economic consequences of discovery (litigation, tarnished reputation, etc.). Perhaps there are economies of scale to auditors as there are to insurers. In particular, larger audit firms might be more efficient (economical) in their detail testing not just because they were more sophisticated than smaller audit firms, but also because as size (wealth) increases, tolerance for risk may increase. There is an interesting inference in the recent UK survey of audit research,[10] that some large firms of auditors are indeed willing systematically to countenance more audit risk than others.

In case (b) the auditor's subjective posterior probability distribution is substantially within the materiality range of the management's assertion of the value of a particular proposition, but the auditor's best point estimate for the proposition differs from the asserted value, p_i^*. Since the difference between the auditor's opinion and management's assertion is, by definition, not material, no adjustment is made and this case is treated as case (a) above. In an auditor's file of working papers an

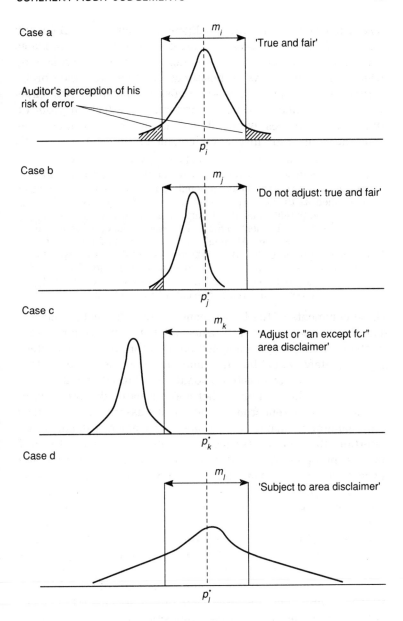

Figure 3.9. The four cases for the auditor in comparing materiality and subjective posterior probability beliefs for particular assertions.

unadjusted errors schedule would be a real-world analogue of this case. However, auditors would need to be wary if too many propositions fell into case (b) because there is a problem of correlation between the propositions. In particular, since profit is a residual measure ('a small difference between two large numbers'), it could arise that the cumulative effect on profit of case (b) differences were all in one direction. Witness the Department of Trade Inspectors' comments on Court Line:

> We are well aware that in accounting matters a considerable degree of individual judgement is required and that it is often possible for properly held, although different, opinions to be maintained as to the correct treatment of individual items. It is, however, apparent that the Court Line Directors consistently exercised their judgement to make disclosed pre-tax profits appear as large as possible. Although we were sympathetic to the arguments presented to us in relation to certain of the specific matters we believe that it is the overall presentation by Court Line that has to be considered in order to assess whether the published Accounts did really present a 'true and fair view'.[11]

These comments of the Department of Trade Inspectors suggest that the concept of overall 'true and fair view' is not just a mechanical one, simply implying that each proposition is materially accurately stated, but 'true and fair view' also requires that assertion of each proposition should be unbiased overall.

In case (c) the auditor's belief about a particular proposition is materially different from management's assertion. In this case if the auditor is unable to persuade management to change the assertion, the auditor issues an area disclaimer in the form of an 'except opinion'. The distinction between 'subject to' and 'except' opinions is made in *Auditing Standard: Qualifications in Audit Reports*.[12]

In case (d) the auditor's subjective posterior probability distribution, despite exhausting the battery of audit procedures, remains too diffuse. Even though the auditor's best point estimate for the proposition may not be materially different from the asserted value (it may even be coincident) the probability of error is so large that the auditor issues a 'subject to' area disclaimer on the grounds that he is unable to satisfy himself as to the material accuracy of the proposition.

In expressing an overall view of the accounts there are three types of report that an auditor can give.

(i)   *An overall true and fair view* which is given when all the
      degrees of belief for all the propositions from which the
      financial statements are constructed are inside the
      acceptable region. That is all propositions are like either
      cases (a) or (b).

(ii) *An area disclaimer* which is given when the degrees of
      belief for the propositions from which the financial
      statements are constructed are mostly inside the accept-
      able region (cases (a) and (b)), except for a few
      propositions subject to the disclaimer which are case
      (c).

(iii) A *total disclaimer* which is given when the number and
      significance of the propositions that are not in the
      acceptable region are such that 'true and fair view' is
      no longer a convenient shorthand for the material
      accuracy of the accounts. An auditor would issue a
      total disclaimer based on the significance of the area
      disclaimers. An illustration of such a report is given in
      Figure 3.10.

3.7 Summary

In an informal way I have given an overview of the main
components of a model of audit judgement. I have distinguished
the fundamental propositions from which the accounts are
assembled, the materiality intervals and the range of values that
they could take. More importantly, I have suggested that audit
judgement about the correct value for a proposition can be
represented by a distribution of probability weights, and be
shown graphically as the area under a curve. Judgement is
quantified by imagining such an area as describing the weighting
attached to each possible value. Provided judgement is coherent,
then the rules and results of probability can be invoked to
elaborate the model. As evidence is collected, so judgement
changes, and the weight attaching to possible values also changes.
I have used some standard results to explain how evidence
changes judgement and have indicated a view of how audit
reporting connects with such a model of judgement. In the next

Whessoe Limited   27 September 1980

Report of the auditors:

To the members of Whessoe Limited

We have audited the accounts on pages ... to ... in accordance with
approved Auditing Standards.

As indicated in note 19 the company has received a claim in respect
of the Qatar contract. The extent of the liability, if any, cannot be
quantified at this stage.

Because of the uncertainty of this matter, we are unable to form an
opinion as to whether the accounts give a true and fair view of the
state of affairs of the company and of the group at 27 September 1980
and of the loss and source and application of funds of the group for
the year then ended.

In other respects the accounts, which have been prepared on the
basis of accounting policies set out on pages ... and ..., in our opinion
comply with the companies Acts 1948 and 1967.

PEAT, MARWICK, MITCHELL & CO.
Chartered Accountants
Darlington
16 December 1980

Figure 3.10.   An example of a qualified audit report.

chapter I use the device of a probability function to explore how
the judgement weighting changes with evidence, which in turn
leads to a practical way of quantifying audit judgement.

Notes and references

1   It is instructive to be aware of the historical context and the
    changing nature of company auditing and its objectives, when
    considering contemporary debates about expectation gaps between
    the professional and lay views of an audit. For the former see: T.A.
    Lee (1972) *Company Auditing: Concepts and Practices*, Chap. 2.
    London: Gee & Co. For a review of the latter see: D. Gwilliam
    (1987) *A Survey of Auditing Research*, Chaps 4 and 5. London:
    Prentice-Hall.
2   T.W. McRae (1982) *A Study of the Application of Statistical*

Sampling to External Auditing, p. 323. London: Institute of Chartered Accountants in England and Wales.

3 McRae, p. 179 (see note 2).
4 The formal analysis of the economics of information is, at its core, based around the exploration of the quantified decision context. See for example: J.S. Demski (1980) *Information Analysis*, New York: Addison-Wesley. For an exposition of management science see: R.L. Winkler (1972) *Introduction to Bayesian Inference and Decision*, New York: Holt, Rinehart Winston.
5 P.G. Moore and H. Thomas (1975) Measuring uncertainty, *Omega*, **III**, 657–672.
6 B. De Finetti (1964) Foresight: its logical laws, its subjective sources. Reprinted in translation in H.E. Kyburg and H.E. Smokler (Eds). *Studies in Subjective Probability*. New York: Wiley.
7 Probability must satisfy many conditions, but it has been found that if three conditions, called axioms, are satisfied, the other conditions that one would require are also satisfied. See for example: B.W. Lindgren (1968) *Statistical Theory*. New York: McMillan.
8 G. Shafer and R. Srivastava (1990) The Bayesian and belief-function formalisms: a general perspective for auditing, *Auditing: A Journal of Practice and Theory*, **9** (Suppl.), 110–137.
9 A. Steele (1984) Another look at the levels of assurance issue in auditing, *Accounting and Business Research*, **14** (54), 147–156.
10 D. Gwilliam and R. Macve (1982) The view from the top on today's auditing revolution, *Accountancy*, **Nov.**, 116–121.
11 Department of Trade Inspectors. Report on published accounts of Court Line, p. 138. London: HMSO.
12 Auditing Practices Committee (1978) *Auditing Standard: Qualifications in Audit Reports*, paragraphs 3 and 4. London: Auditing Practices Committee.

Chapter 4

Implementation and the Equivalent Prior Sample

4.1 Introduction

The approach I have sketched has been advocated by audit researchers for over 20 years.[1] It enables auditors to combine their past experience, knowledge about the client 'auditor's nose' and so on together with sampling evidence in an explicit and defensible way. The benefits lie in reduced sample sizes, lower audit costs and more efficient risk management.[2] The critical step lies in quantification. The non-sampled evidence needs to be quantified before it can be combined.

Whilst there is a very large literature in psychology and in management sciences,[3] research in this area with practising auditors is in its infancy.[4] There has been a great deal of laboratory work, but at the outset an important caveat is that much work remains to be done in realistic settings. Two factors that are apparent from the work which has been done to date are the potential profitability of the approach, and the importance of training.

Even experts experience difficulty in quantifying judgement. We are generally over-confident, tending to believe that we are more certain than we really are.[5] We tend to use rules of thumb and heuristics which bias our judgements.[6] We are generally poor intuitive statisticians—different techniques for quantifying judgement lead to different measures; we are sensitive to different apparatus and to how problems are framed; we find reconciliation of different estimates stressful and tiring; we allow our own personal attitudes to gambling and risk to confuse our assessments; we are not very good at distinguishing a 1 in 10 chance from a 1 in 20 chance from a 1 in a 100 chance (i.e. probabilities of 0.1, 0.05, 0.01, or 0.9, 0.95, 0.99 are not well handled). However, with training and with 'user-friendly' decision-support tools (such as Novick's (1971) Bayesian computer-assisted data analysis (CADA) package[7]) these problems have been overcome in experimental settings.

In this chapter I set out the equivalent prior sample (EQPS) method of quantifying non-sampled evidence. Of all the methods[8] which have been advocated and tested this has been found to have considerable intuitive appeal in the audit context.[9] The method requires the auditor to think of his or her subjective beliefs as equivalent to a hypothetical sample result. In order to understand how a computer package is used as a decision aid in this application, it is first necessary to explain the logical basis for incorporating sample evidence with prior beliefs.

The explanation is set out using a slightly artificial example. The example is used to demonstrate the significance of a key result obtained by Thomas Bayes (1714) from which this approach to the interpretation of evidence (Bayesian analysis) derives its name. The result leads to a natural means of quantifying judgement using a standard family of weight functions for a proportion—the β distributions. The equivalent prior sample method is a technique for choosing the most appropriate β distribution with which to quantify prior judgement. Having set out the agenda for this chapter, the first task is to model the exact process by which prior judgements become 'massed' from evidence.

4.2 Example: a bad debt provision

A company is owed 10 000 small debts. Since none of the debts is individually significant, the provision for doubtful debts is based on the proportion of the year-end debts which are envisaged to be doubtful. In the past this has varied between 3% and 15%. The proportion is only ever estimated to the nearest 3%. At this point of the exposition it is assumed that the auditor has in some way quantified his prior judgement as shown in Table 4.1.

Table 4.1. The auditor's quantification of his prior judgement.

Percentage of doubtful debts	3	6	9	12	15
Prior judgement weight	0.20	0.40	0.20	0.10	0.10

One can check that these judgement weights are coherent, by summing them to one. The company have set up a provision based on a percentage rate of 9%. In order to decide whether it is a fair provision the auditor takes a sample of 30 accounts, and using a circularization finds zero doubtful accounts. What should the auditor's revised judgement be in the light of such evidence? Should the auditor collect more evidence? What should a true and fair provision be?

Whilst retaining some elements of realism the example (based on McRae[10]) is as simplified as appropriate. The prior judgements have been already quantified in order to focus on how they interact with evidence, as a preliminary to demonstrating how they can be more naturally represented. The natural representation, as we shall see, is more realistic, giving weight in a continuous way to any proportion between 0 and 100%, rather than only the values $A = 3\%$, $B = 6\%$, $C = 9\%$, $D = 12\%$ and $E = 15\%$.

4.3 Likelihoods

The judgement weights are represented by the area under a curve. The prior judgements about the proportion of doubtful

debts can be represented as shown in Figure 3.4. To explore how
sample evidence will change these weights, we consider first the
situation in which it is possible for an auditor to gain unambiguous
evidence about the bad debt proportion. Suppose for instance that
the accounts were being drawn up a long while after the year-end
and that all the debts had been settled and all the defaults defaulted
in the intervening period. Rather than having to forecast the
proportion of bad debts, the auditor could gain unambiguous
evidence. There are a set of five possible signals that this
unambiguous source could give in this case:

Z_A under 3%,
Z_B between 3% and under 6%,
Z_C 6% and under 9%,
Z_D between 9% and under 12%, and
Z_E 12% or more.

Suppose the signal was Z_A (under 3%). This would occur with
some probability $P(Z_A)$. However, among the five states (A to E)
it would unambiguously identify A. The way that a signal identifies
state is known as the *likelihood* of the signal. The likelihood for
each state for the signal Z_A is given in Table 4.2. The likelihood
of a signal is the conditional probability of observing the signal
given the state. The effect of such a signal would be to mass all
the judgement weight at A. The term 'signal' is here used to
denote any data or audit evidence.

Now consider the more usual case where data are ambiguous
and associated to some degree with several states. In the present
example, observing zero bad debts in a debtors circularization
of 30 is such an ambiguous signal. From a sample of size 30,

Table 4.2. The likelihood for each state for the signal Z_A.

State	Proportion, p	Likelihood of Z_A, $P(Z_A)$
A	0.03	$P(Z_A)$
B	0.06	0
C	0.09	0
D	0.12	0
E	0.15	0

Table 4.3. The likelihood for each state for the signal Z_A when $P(Z_0)$ = $(1-p)^{30}$.

State	Proportion, p	Likelihood of $P(Z_0) = (1-p)^{30}$
A	0.03	0.4010
B	0.06	0.1563
C	0.09	0.0591
D	0.12	0.0216
E	0.15	0.0076

zero bad debts is one of a set of a possible 31 signals (e.g. Z_1 observing one bad debt, or Z_2 two bad debts, or Z_3 three bad debts, and so on), each of which is ambiguous. The likelihood of zero bad debts out of a sample of 30 is the conditional probability of obtaining this result given the state. If the proportion of bad debts is p, then the probability of this result[11] is $P(Z_0) = (1-p)^{30}$. The likelihood for each state at this stage is given in Table 4.3. It is evident that observing a sample of 0 out of 30 is more likely to occur if the proportion of bad debts is low rather than high; however, the evidence is not clear cut since there is some probability of getting this result from each state. We now have for each proportion both our prior judgement weights, and

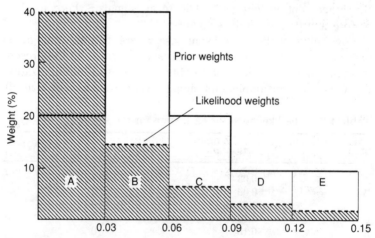

Figure 4.1. Prior judgement and likelihood.

the likelihood of our audit evidence. These judgement weights are represented in Figure 4.1. Our task is to combine them, revising our prior judgements taking into account the likelihood of our audit evidence.

4.4 Bayes' theorem

The postulate of coherence requires that prior probability assessments are revised in the face of sample evidence according to Bayes' theorem:

$$P(A \mid Z) = \frac{P(A)\,P(Z \mid A)}{P(Z)}$$

In its simplest form Bayes' theorem[12] is merely a statement about conditional probabilities. The probability of A given or conditional on Z can be calculated from the probability of Z given A, and the unconditional probability of A and the unconditional probability of Z.

A betting derivation would be as follows. If an auditor has a judgement $P(A \text{ and } Z)$ for an event A and Z occurring, and a judgement $P(Z)$ for an event Z occurring, then once told that event Z has occurred then the judgement for event A should be revised as follows: $P(A|Z) = P(A \text{ and } Z)/P(Z)$. An equivalent rule is: $P(A \text{ and } Z) = P(A|Z) \times P(Z)$. Suppose, for example, that the auditor's judgement does not obey this rule, say $P(A \text{ and } Z) < P(A|Z) \times P(Z)$. Then we could bet $\pounds P(A \text{ and } Z)$ on A and Z, with a bet $\pounds P(A|Z)\,P(Z)$ against Z. If event Z occurs we bet $\pounds(1 - P(A|Z))$ against A.

There are three ways in which things could turn out, and in each case we win $\pounds P(A|Z)\,P(Z) - P(A \text{ and } Z)$.

(i) Both events A and Z occur, in which case we win $\pounds(1 - P(A \text{ and } Z)$ but lose $\pounds P(A|Z)\,(1 - P(Z))$ on the bet against Z. We also lose $\pounds(1 - P(A|Z))$ on the bet against A after event Z has occurred. Thus the net winnings are:

$\pounds(1 - P(A \text{ and } Z) - P(A|Z)\,(1 - P(Z)) - (1 - P(A|Z)))$
=
$\pounds P(A|Z)P(Z) - P(A \text{ and } Z)$.

(ii) Z occurs, but A does not. In this case we lose $£P$(A and Z). We also lose on the bet against Z an amount of $£P$(A$|$Z) $(1 - P$(Z)). However, we win the bet against A after Z has occurred, and get $£P$(A$|$Z). The net winnings are:

$£(-P$(A and Z) $- P$(A$|$Z) $(1 - P$(Z)) $+ P$(A$|$Z)) $=$
$£P$(A$|$Z)P(Z) $- P$(A and Z)

(iii) Z does not occur. In this case we lose on the bet A and Z the sum of $£P$(A and Z) but we win P(Z)P(A$|$Z) on the bet against Z. The net winnings are again:

$£P$(A$|$Z)P(Z) $- P$(A and Z)

In the case where the auditor does not condition his judgement according to this relationship and P(A and Z) $> P$(A$|$Z) $\times P$(Z), then we can reverse all bets and net a certain (but hypothetical) $£P$(A and Z) $- P$(A$|$Z) $\times P$(Z). This argument establishes that, in order to be coherent, judgements should be revised as:

$$P(\text{A}|\text{Z}) = \frac{P(\text{A and Z})}{P(\text{Z})}$$

The last step in the derivation is to substitute the numerator of the ratio by using similar arguments to establish that P(A and Z) $= P$(A) $\times P$(Z$|$A).

A standard textbook application of the result is shown in Figure 4.2.

At one level Bayes' theorem is a mere component of an introductory statistics course. However, the importance of the result can be seen from identifying:

(i) P(A$|$Z) the probability of A conditional on Z as the *posterior* judgement weight we give to state A after we have observed the evidence or signal Z;

(ii) P(A) is the *prior* judgement weight we give to state A, before evidence Z is collected; and

(iii) P(Z$|$A) is the *likelihood* of the evidence Z given state A.

Bayes' theorem can be more memorably restated as:

posterior $\propto$ prior $\times$ likelihood.

We do not need to bother with P(Z) since it is only a rescaling constant.[13]

An auditor estimates that there is a 70% probability that a potential client is a going concern. In order to confirm this prior judgement he uses a Z score bankruptcy prediction model which gives a 'clean bill of health' for the company. The Z score model is not infallible. However, experience has shown that if the company really is a going concern, then the probability that the Z score test result will be favourable is 0.9. If the company is going to fail within 12 months then the Z score test result will be favourable only with probability 0.2. Some 69% of Z-score tests are favourable. Having received the 'signal', this additional evidence, what should be the auditor's revised probability of a going concern in the light of this test result?

Solution
  Let A = going concern $P(A) = 0.70$
  Let Z = favourable Z score $P(Z) = 0.69$

  Conditional probability $P(Z|A) = 0.90$

Hence $P(A|Z) = \dfrac{0.70 \times 0.90}{0.69} = 0.91$

Thus the probability judgement weight should be increased from the original 70% to 91%.

Figure 4.2. An illustration of the application of Bayes' theorem.

Table 4.4. The auditor's quantification of his posterior judgement.

State	Proportion, p	Prior	Likelihood	Prior × likelihood	Posterior*
A	0.03	0.20	0.4010	0.0802	0.5092
B	0.06	0.40	0.1563	0.0625	0.3968
C	0.09	0.20	0.0591	0.0118	0.0749
D	0.12	0.10	0.0216	0.0022	0.0140
E	0.15	0.10	0.0076	0.0008	0.0051
Total				0.1575	1.000

* Posterior is prior × likelihood rescaled so that it sums to one, by dividing through by the sum 0.1575.

Returning to the example of a bad debt provision, to revise our prior judgements taking into account our audit evidence, we take the product of our priors with our likelihoods and rescale as shown in Table 4.4.

The answer to our first question 'What should the auditor's revised judgement be in the light of this evidence?' can be represented as in Figure 4.3. The shape of the prior judgement weight curve has changed in the light of evidence. The judgement weights have become more concentrated. As common sense suggests, the probability of lower bad debt provision has increased, since no bad debts were discovered in the circularization.

The debtors circularization has not removed all doubt, which leads to our second question: 'Should the auditor collect more evidence?' In the model outlined in Chapter 3, deciding on the sufficiency of evidence involves comparing the acceptable range or materiality interval with the area under this judgement curve. Suppose for illustrative purposes that the materiality interval has been set to the nearest 3%; this situation is depicted in Figure 4.4.

It is apparent that there is a good deal of judgement weight outside the acceptable interval. The auditor attaches a probability weight of 0.5092 to a provision as low as 3%, and even some very small probability (0.0051) that the provision is understated.

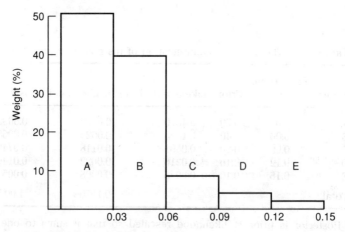

Figure 4.3. Posterior judgements.

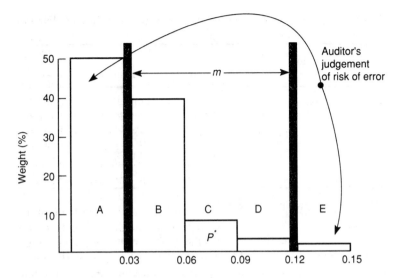

Figure 4.4. Posterior judgement weights and materiality.

Table 4.5. The likelihood of a single debtor out of 10 being identified as being in dispute.

State	Proportion, p	Likelihood, $10p(1-p)^9$
A	0.03	0.2281
B	0.06	0.3438
C	0.09	0.3851
D	0.12	0.3798
E	0.15	0.3474

In this situation the auditor decides (despite the expense) to take a further sample of 10 debtors to circulate in order to test his view that a provision based on 9% is too generous. This time in the sample of 10, a single debtor is identified as being in dispute and is doubtful. The likelihood[14] of this result is given by $10p(1-p)^9$ and is shown in Table 4.5.

The previous *posterior* beliefs can be treated as *prior* beliefs needing to be up-dated in the light of the additional evidence, exactly as before (see Table 4.6). It can be seen that the judgement weights are shifted again, in the light of the additional evidence.

Table 4.6. The previous posterior beliefs up-dated in the light of additional evidence can be treated as prior beliefs.

State	Proportion, p	Prior	Likelihood	Prior × likelihood	Posterior*
A	0.03	0.5092	0.2281	11.6149	0.4026
B	0.06	0.3968	0.3438	13.6420	0.4729
C	0.09	0.0749	0.3851	2.8844	0.1000
D	0.12	0.0140	0.3798	0.5317	0.0184
E	0.15	0.0051	0.3474	0.1772	0.0061
Total				28.8502	1.0000

* Rescaled by dividing by 28.8502.

The attractions of the formal approach we are developing are that it allows us defensibly and logically to interpret the audit evidence. It allows us to make risk statements which mean something. At this stage the audit work could be summarized by a statement that there is a 60% chance (0.4729 + 0.1000 + 0.0184) that the proportion of doubtful debts is 9% within the materiality limits of 3%. This statement means that this judgement is equivalent to a bet on which we would give odds of 60:40.

With a little more work we will soon be able to answer the third question: 'What should a true and fair provision be?' This question is left to the next chapter.

Our example illustrates the Bayesian revision process by which prior judgements get 'massed' by evidence. Understanding this process is the key to the easiest way of representing these prior judgements in the first place.

4.5 Conjugate priors

As has been stated previously, the Achilles' heel of the present approach lies in the quantification of a non-sample evidence and the formulation of a prior. Since this can only be done approximately, a practical approach is to have a selection of standard or template priors available, and to pick the one which most nearly matches the actual situation. These standard priors are referred to by statisticians as 'natural conjugate priors'. They ideally should be analytically tractable, being easy to program, easy to interpret, easily described and rich in shapes so that there is a good chance of expressing prior information. It would be convenient if they were a closed family, that is if the prior is a member of a conjugate family then so is the posterior. This will make revision of judgements for sequential samples easier. For modelling judgement about proportions, such as the proportion of errors in a system, or the proportion of debts that are doubtful, the β distributions form a family of conjugate priors.

The β distributions are a rich family of weight functions indexed by two parameters (a and b). For illustration, when $a = 1$ and $b = 1$ the shape of the β function is flat (Figure 4.5). This is the most diffuse prior and corresponds to the situation in which one has no confidence in one's prior judgement. Each proportion is equally weighted. When an auditor is unwilling to quantify his prior judgement this is the appropriate prior to choose.

As the parameter b increases, the shape of the β distribution skews to the right, moving through a triangular shape to increasingly steep exponential curves (Figure 4.6). The effect of this is to give more weight to lower proportions. Typically, in compliance testing and attribute testing auditors are looking at situations with low error rates, for which such members of the β family might be appropriate.

When the parameter a increases, the family includes shapes which have modes away from zero. When $a=b$ symmetrical distributions are produced. When $a > b$ the distributions are skewed to the left. Some of the variety of β density functions which have a mode of 0.8 are shown in Figure 4.7.

The formula for any member of the β distribution family is

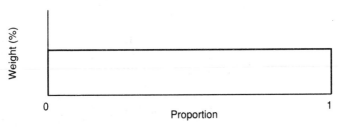

Figure 4.5. The β function when $a = 1$ and $b = 1$.

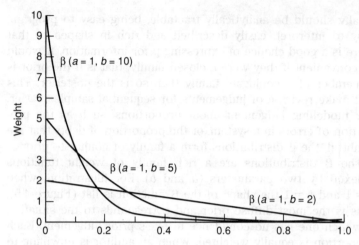

Figure 4.6. The β function when $a = 1$ and $b = 2$, $b = 5$ or $b = 10$.

$$f(p) = k\, p^{a-1}\, (1-p)^{b-1}$$

where k is the constant of proportionality, so that the area under the judgement curve is 1. That is

$$\int_0^1 f(p)\,\mathrm{d}p = \int_0^1 kp^{a-1}(1-p)^{b-1} = 1$$

from which

$$1/k = \int_0^1 p^{a-1}(1-p)^{b-1}\,\mathrm{d}p$$

When a and b are integers this integral simplifies to

$$k = \frac{(a+b-1)!}{(a-1)!(b-1)!}$$

When a and b are not integers k can be found by numerical methods, for example by using Simpson's rule.[13]

If for illustration we choose $a = 2$ and $b = 23$, then the prior function would be described by the area under a curve

$$f(p) = 552p\,(1-p)^{22}$$

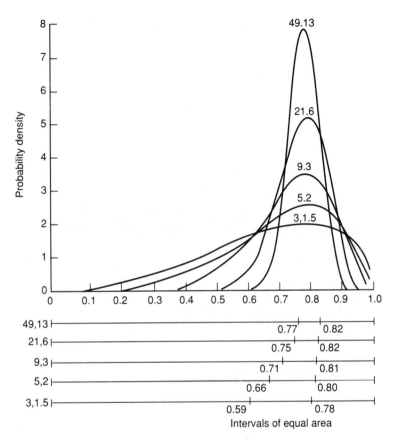

Figure 4.7. β density functions having a mode of 0.8.

This particular curve has a 50% judgement interval between the proportions 0.04 and 0.10. In other words, if this particular β function adequately represents background knowledge then a range estimate in which one is 50% confident would be a bad debt proportion of between 4% and 10%. This particular curve gives almost (but not quite) zero judgement weight to bad debt proportions above 25%. Since it is a skewed shape the mean proportion of 8% does not equal the modal proportion of 4.3%. The median proportion of 6.9% falls in between the two (this variety of summary measures makes the question of what would be a point estimate for a true and fair provision interesting). In general, the descriptive statistics for the β distribution are given as follows:

$$\text{mean} \quad = \frac{a}{b+a}$$

$$\text{mode} \quad = \frac{a-1}{a+b-2}$$

$$\text{median} \quad \simeq 2/3 \text{ mean} + 1/3 \text{ mode}$$

$$\text{variance} = \frac{ab}{(a+b)^2(a+b+1)}$$

In our example about the bad debt provision, rather than asking the auditor to quantify his prior judgement for five discrete percentages (A = 3%, B = 6%, C = 9%, D = 12% and E = 15%), we could use some method[16] to get the auditors to identify this particular β distribution as being a close enough weight function to model his prior beliefs about the proportion. The particular method advocated here relies on the way in which the β distribution changes as it incorporates evidence.

4.6 Incorporating audit evidence

Forming a defensible judgement about a proportion is an important problem in auditing. It arises in attribute sampling (What proportion of the population possess this attribute?); in compliance testing (What proportion of items do not comply with the procedures?); it can also arise in substantive testing (What is the total error in an account balance?) when estimates are needed of the proportion of items in error as well as their amount. In each of these cases a representative selection from the whole population is checked, some of which will have the characteristic of interest and the rest will not. Such evidence gathering is like coin tossing where, provided that the probability of a head is a constant (p) from toss to toss, and the tosses are independent of each other, then we can work out the *likelihood* of our results. For example, in a sequence of 10 tosses, the result TTHTTTHHHH (T, tails; H, heads) would have a probability which depends on p of $(1-p) \times (1-p) \times p \times (1-p) \times (1-p)$

$\times$ $(1-p)$ $\times$ p $\times$ p $\times$ p $\times$ p or $p^5(1-p)^5$. For any sequence of length n and x 'successes' the likelihood would be $p^x(1-p)^{n-x}$.

This result requires that the proportion p is constant. In the audit context this strictly implies some factors about the process of collecting evidence:

(i) the selection is random, with each member of the population having the same chance of being picked for examination;

(ii) the population is large (as a rule of thumb, 20 times larger than the sample size); and

(iii) sampling is with replacement (although this is never done in practice).

That said, the likelihood of observing x items with a particular characteristic in an audit sample of size n depends on the proportion p of the population with the characteristic. We write

$$L(p) \propto p^x(1-p)^{n-x}$$

where the $\propto$ sign is equivalent to an equals sign, but means that the left-hand term is only proportional to the right hand term, and differs from the right-hand term in the equation by a multiplying constant.

With prior beliefs about p, we incorporate our evidence using Bayes' theorem that posterior $\propto$ prior $\times$ likelihood. This gives

$$\text{posterior} \propto p^{a-1} (1-p)^{b-1} \times p^x (1-p)^{n-x}$$

or, collecting items together,

$$\text{posterior} \propto p^{a+x-1} (1-p)^{b+n-x-1}$$

It can be seen why the β family is such a convenient set of functions for modelling prior judgement about a proportion, because the posterior beliefs are also modelled by a β distribution. The posterior β distribution will have parameters $(a+x)$ and $(b+n-x)$, where n is the sample size and x is the number of 'successes' found.

Returning yet again to our example of the bad debt provision, a debtors circularization of $n = 30$ and $x = 0$, and the prior beliefs about the proportion of bad debts now modelled by a β distribution with parameters $a = 2$ and $b = 23$. Then the posterior beliefs will be modelled by a β distribution with parameters $a = 2 + 0 = 2$, and $b = 23 + 30 = 53$. This has the equation 2862

$p(1-p)^{52}$, a modal proportion of 1.88% and a mean proportion of 3.64%.

The second sample of debtors, with one identified as doubtful ($n = 10$, $x = 1$), is incorporated in the same way. The beliefs are now modelled by β distribution with parameters $a = 2 + 1 = 3$ and $b = 53 + 10 - 1 = 62$. This has an equation $kp^2(1-p)^{61}$, and a mode of $(3-1)/(3+62-2) = 3.175\%$ which is a low error rate. The mean proportion of errors consistent with these revised beliefs is $3/(3+62) = 4.615\%$. The fact that the mean is greater than the mode indicates that the judgement distribution has a skew towards higher error rates. These changes in judgement weights are shown in Figure 4.8.

As before, the posterior judgement curve summarizes the prior non-sampling beliefs and the audit evidence allowing risk judgements to be made. In terms of implementing the model outlined in Chapter 3, the area under the curve in the materiality ranges from 6% to 12% quantifies the confidence that the auditor has in management's assertion of a provision based on 9%.

This model is behaving in an intuitively sensible way, balancing audit judgement and audit evidence. In the first debtors circularization no doubtful debts were identified. Very frequently auditors

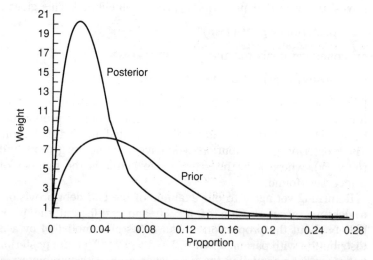

Figure 4.8. The β distributions for: prior, $a = 2$ and $b = 23$; posterior, $a = 2$ and $b = 53$.

take such samples and do not discover any errors, because the proportion of errors in most situations is very low. However, the auditor does not jump to a conclusion that the population is error free; rather the conclusion is a balance between prior judgement and the sample result. The prior mean is $a/(b + a)$, so the posterior mean will be $(a + x)/(b + a + n)$. This posterior mean may equivalently be expressed as

$$w \left(\frac{a}{b + a} \right) + (1 - w) \left(\frac{x}{n} \right)$$

where

$$w = \frac{a + b}{a + b + n}$$

That is the posterior mean is a weighted average of the prior mean $a/(b + a)$ and the sample proportion (x/n). As more and more evidence is collected and n becomes larger and larger, the weight (w) which is attached to the prior mean becomes smaller and smaller. This is again intuitively logical. For small amounts of data prior judgement is important, but as evidence accumulates these prior beliefs become much less significant.

4.7 Equivalent prior sample

Using a β distribution as a conjugate prior makes revising judgements very easy. In summary this can be expressed as

Prior		Evidence		Posterior
β distribution	+	sample size n,	$\rightarrow$	β distribution
(a,b)		x with characteristics,		$(a+x,\ b+n-x)$
		$(n-x)$ without		
		characteristics		

This result also provides us with a way of conceiving of our non-sampling prior judgement as being equivalent to a hypothetical audit sample. From our earlier discussion, we said that a β distribution with the parameters $a=1$ and $b=1$ corresponds to a uniform distribution, in which every proportion has the same weight. This was the prior to choose if one had no confidence in one's non-sampling judgement, and wished to rely exclusively on sampling evidence to sustain the opinion. If one started from this ignorance prior and took a sample of size $(a+b-2)$, of whom $(a-1)$ had the characteristic and $(b-1)$ did not, then the posterior would be a β function with parameters a and b. In other words, the prior beliefs about a proportion are equivalent to having already taken a sample size of $(a+b-2)$. This then is the technique of the equivalent prior sample for choosing a conjugate distribution to model non-sampling information.

Software exists for quantifying judgement using exactly this approach. The interactive program CADA proceeds by asking for the modal or most likely value for the proportion, and then how many sample observations this point estimate is worth. It then feeds back some data on the shape of the member of the β family selected, so that the inputs may be revised and, if necessary, a more appropriate member chosen.

An extract[17] from CADA showing how an investigator settles on a β distribution with parameters $a = 149.5$ and $b = 50.5$ as most nearly representing judgement prior to sampling is shown in Figure 4.9. This package was developed over a decade ago for use on a main-frame computer in a teaching and research environment. It has not yet been adapted for use on microcomputers.

Blocker and Robertson[18] have described an alternative program for choosing a member of the family β distributions to quantify prior judgements, which they use in a classroom setting. The student auditor is asked for a prior estimate of the error rate, for example 5%. The degree of certainty about this prior estimate is then not specified numerically as in the equivalent prior sample method, instead a qualitative choice is made 'not so sure', or 'sure', or 'very sure'. Corresponding to these three categories the program assigns a variance to the prior mean. Using the results given earlier that the mean is $a/(b+a)$ and the variance is $ab/((a+b)^2(a+b+1))$ the program calculates the values of a and b that most nearly represent the judgement prior to sampling.

If the prior estimate of the error rate provided by the student auditor is the mean error rate μ, and the value assigned to the variance corresponding to 'not so sure', 'sure', or 'very sure' is denoted as v then the Blocker and Robertson procedure will choose a β distribution as follows:

$$a = \mu \, (\mu \, (1-\mu)-v)/v$$
$$b = (1-\mu)(\mu(1-\mu)-v)/v$$

Within the class of conjugate prior β distributions serving as convenient templates for the weights in prior judgement, the procedure restricts itself to a subset defined by a choice of only three possible values for v.

An alternative procedure for selecting an appropriate member of the β family suggested by Pratt *et al.*[19] uses the normal distribution as an approximation to the β distribution. For large values of a and b (in practice for $(a+b) > 10$), the area under the β distribution between 0 and some value x, is approximately the same as the area under a unit normal distribution between $-\infty$ and z, where the value of z is given by

$$z = 2[x(b-1/3)]^{\frac{1}{2}} - 2[(1-x)(a-1/3)]^{\frac{1}{2}}$$

The unit normal distribution is a symmetrical bell-shaped curve the formula for which is

$$f(y) = k \, \exp \, (y^2/2)$$

for real values of y. It has a mean of zero and a standard deviation of one.

The constant of proportionality k is $(2\pi)^{-0.5} = 0.39894$. The problem of finding the area under a β distribution is thus transformed into the equivalent problem:

$$k \int_0^x p^{a-1} \, (1-p)^{b-1} \, \mathrm{d}p = (2\pi)^{-0.5} \int_{-\infty}^z \exp \, (y^2/2) \mathrm{d}y$$

The solution to the right-hand-side of the above equation is given as the area under the curve which is presented in tables of the normal distribution.

For example, an auditor models his judgement about the proportion of attributes in a population using a β distribution having the parameters $a = 5$ and $b = 20$. What is the judgement weight that should be given to an assertion that the proportion of the population with the attribute is in fact under 30%?

Computer-assisted data analysis

If you wish an explanation type 1, else type 0,
?
1

> [A question mark indicates that a response is required from the analyst who in this case desires a listing of available routines.]

This packet of programs provides a grounding in the fundamentals of Bayesian methods of statistical inference. These routines are designed to guide the researcher who has only a minimal acquaintance with Bayesian methods, step-by-step through a complete Bayesian analysis. A list of the routines follows:

1   Prior β-binomial model
2   posterior β-binomial model
3   prior two-parameter normal-marginal distribution of r standard deviation
4   prior two-parameter normal-conditional distribution for mean
5   posterior two-parameter normal
6   prior m-group proportions
7   posterior m-group proportions
8   evaluate Student-distribution
9   evaluate β-distribution
10 evaluate inverse χ-distribution
11 evaluate normal distribution

If you want to run one of the above routines, type its number. Otherwise, type a zero.
?
1

Bayesian statistical analysis for the β-binomial model

This program will assist you in specifying a prior distribution in the β class for a binomial parameter (proportion), π, after arriving at a satisfactory specification for the prior, sample data from your experiment will be used to compute the posterior distribution.

Considering your prior information, what do you feel to be the most probable value for π? π must be greater than 0.05 and less than 0.95.
?
0.75

Figure 4.9. An extract from CADA showing how a β distribution with $a = 149.5$ and $b = 50.5$ is obtained as most nearly representing the judgement prior to sampling.

Now considering your prior information as if it were the results of an experiment of sample size (*m*), how many sample observations do you feel your prior information to be worth? This *m* value is the amount of weight that will be given to your prior information and must be 6 or greater.
?
25
Your model estimate of π = 0.750 and the *m* value 25.000 you selected imply that you would be willing to give even odds that the true value of π will be in the 50% highest density region (hdr) credibility interval which extends from 0.688 to 0.806.

Please consider this interval, it may or may not be satisfactory to you. You may increase it by selecting a small *m* value, or decrease it by selecting a larger *m* value. However, any change will affect the relative weight you will be giving to your prior information.

If you are satisfied with the interval, please type a zero, otherwise, type your new *m* value.
?
50

> [The investigator places little probability on the belief that the true proportion lies outside the interval (0.688, 0.806). Therefore, incrementing *m* is clearly indicated.]

Your modal estimate of π 0.750 and the *m* value 50.000 you selected imply that you would be willing to give odds that the true value of π will be in the 50% hdr credibility interval which extends from 0.707 to 0.790.

If you are satisfied with the interval, please type a zero, otherwise, type your new *m* value.
?
100

Your modal estimate of π 0.750 and the *m* value 100.000 you selected imply that you would be willing to give even odds that the true value of π will be in the 50% hdr credibility interval which extends from 0.720 to 0.779.

If you are satisfied with the interval, please type a zero, otherwise, type your new *m* value.
?
150

Figure 4.9. *continued.*

[When evaluating these intervals, the reader must keep in mind that they are 50% hdrs. This means, of course, that once you select one of these even-odds abetting intervals, you must be willing to let someone else select which side of the bet he wishes to take. You must be indifferent which betting whether the true proportion is within or outside the interval chosen. With this in mind, our administrator rejects the above interval as too broad and again increments his *m* value.]

Your modal estimate of π 0.750 and the *m* value 150.000 you selected imply that you would be willing to give even odds that the true value of π will be in the 50% hdr credibility interval which extends from 0.726 to 0.773.

If you are satisfied with the interval, please type a zero, otherwise, type your new *m* value.
?
200

[Our investigator is convinced that even this interval is too large and increments *m* again.]

Your modal estimate of π 0.750 and the *m* value of 200.000 you selected imply that you would be willing to give even odds that the true value of π will be in the 50% hdr credibility interval which extends from 0.729 to 0.770.

If you are satisfied with the interval, please type a zero, otherwise, type your new *m* value.
?
0

[Although our investigator would like the 50% hdr to be slightly tighter, he recognizes that the last 50 hypothetical observations did not significantly change his interval estimate and that additional changes will require more hypothetical observations than he is willing to specify. Therefore, he decided to accept this as a reasonable description of his prior beliefs about the proportion.]

Your prior distribution for π is a β distribution with a mode of 0.750 a mean of 0.747 and a standard deviation of 0.031. The 50% hdr credibility interval extends from 0.729 to 0.770 it has parameters 149.500 and 50.500.

If you wish to respecify your estimate of π, please type that estimate, otherwise, type a 0.
?
0

Figure 4.9. *continued.*

If you want to see any other hdr, type the percent desired, type it as a decimal, for example, a 75% hdr would be 0.75, otherwise, type a zero.
?
0.99

> [As a final check on his prior, our administrator decides to look at the 99% hdr.]

Your modal estimate of π is 0.750 and m is 200.00. The 99% hdr extends from 0.666 to 0.823.

If you want to see any other hdr, type the percent desired, type it as a decimal, for example, a 75% hdr would be 0.75, otherwise, type a zero.
?
0

> [Looking at this interval, he feels comfortable with the assertion that almost all of his probability lies between 0.666 and 0.823. Satisfied that a $\beta(149.5, 50.5)$ adequately describes his prior beliefs, our investigator is now ready to collect some data. Going to the files, our investigator randomly selects 100 items to test and finds that 77 of the 100 items have the property being investigated. He is now ready to evaluate his posterior.]

Do you want to run a posterior analysis?
If you do then type a one, otherwise, type a zero.
?
1

This part of the program will combine your prior distribution with the sample data, and describe the posterior distribution, please type in the two parameters from your prior, in order, enter first parameter, please.
?
149.5

Enter second parameter, please.
?
50.5

Please type in the number of observations in your sample.
?
100

Finally, please type in the number of successes in the sample.
?
77

The posterior distribution for π is a β distribution with a mode of 0.757 a mean of 0.755 and a standard deviation of 0.025. It has parameters 226.500 and 73.500 a 50% hdr credibility interval extends from 0.740 to 0.773.

Figure 4.9. *continued.*

The formulation $\int_0^{0.30} p^4(1-p)^{19}\,dp$

is transformed using

$$z = 2[0.3(20-1/3)]^{\frac{1}{2}} - 2[0.7(5-1/3)]^{\frac{1}{2}} = 1.2432$$

From tables of the normal distribution the area under the curve to the left of $z = 1.2432$ is 89.25%. Thus there is about a 90% chance that the population has less than 30% of a particular attribute. There is a one in ten chance that the proportion exceeds 30%.

The equivalence between the unit or standard normal distribution and the β distribution is only approximate, particularly as β distributions are only symmetrical when they have a mean of 0.5 and the parameters a and b are equal. The unit normal distribution does have known fractiles, and it is this feature which the fractile assessment procedure of Pratt *et al.*[19] uses to find an appropriate β to quantify prior judgement. The values of z that represent the first quartile, the median, and the third quartile of the unit normal found from tables of the distribution are $(-0.675, 0, 0.675)$.

The auditor specifies quartiles of his prior judgement distribution, say q_1, q_2 and q_3. It follows from the normal approximation to the β distribution that

$$-0.675 = 2\,[q_1(b-1/3)]^{\frac{1}{2}} - 2\,[(1-q_1)(a-1/3)]^{\frac{1}{2}}$$
$$0 = 2\,[q_2(b-1/3)]^{\frac{1}{2}} - 2[(1-q_2)(a-1/3)]^{\frac{1}{2}}$$
$$+0.675 = 2\,[q_3(b-1/3)]^{\frac{1}{2}} - 2[(1-q_3)(a-1/3)]^{\frac{1}{2}}$$

All that is necessary to choose a β distribution is to decide on the values for the quartiles. With given values for q_1, q_2 and q_3 there are three equations to provide the unknown values of the two parameters a and b. The procedure will only approximately find values of a and b to reproduce specified quartiles and some adjustment may be needed.[20] When an auditor specifies the three quartiles of his prior distribution, approximate values of a and b are given by:

$$a = cq_2 + 1/3$$
$$b = c(1-q_2) + 1/3$$

where

$$c = 0.057 \ (d_1{}^{-1} + d_3{}^{-1})$$

and

$$d_1 = \{[q_2(1-q_1)]^{0.5} - [q_1(1-q_2)]^{0.5}\}^2$$
$$d_3 = \{[q_2(1-q_3)]^{0.5} - [q_3(1-q_2)]^{0.5}\}^2$$

For an illustration of this approach, suppose that an auditor is seeking to quantify his judgement about the proportion of stock items that have been mispriced. His feeling is that there is a 25% judgement weight to give to an error rate of less than 4%. The median error rate, which is as likely as not to be exceeded, is 6%. The upper quartile is 10%. There is only a 25% chance he would like to assign to an error rate of over 10%. Using $q_1 = 0.04$, $q_2 = 0.06$ and $q_3 = 0.10$ the values of a and b would be found by:

$$d_1 = ((0.06(1-0.04))^{0.5} - (0.04(1-0.06))^{0.5})^2$$

$$d_1 = 0.00212$$

$$d_3 = ((0.06(1-0.1))^{0.5} - (0.1(1-0.06))^{0.5})^2$$

$$d_3 = 0.00551$$

$$c = 0.057 \left[\frac{1}{0.00212} + \frac{1}{0.00551} \right]$$

$$c = 37.23$$

$$a = 37.23 \times 0.06 + 0.333$$

$$a = 2.57$$

$$b = 37.23 \ (1-0.06) + 0.333$$

$$b = 35.33$$

In this case one might take the prior β distribution as $a = 2$, $b = 35$. From the discussion of equivalent prior samples, the auditor's judgement in this illustration is equivalent to having started from ignorance, tested a sample of 37 and found two errors.

The virtue of using an analytical procedure to find a β distribution is somewhat marred in this case by the complexity of the formulae. An inelegant but effective routine based on the mode and the upper and lower quartiles is set out in Figure 4.10. The program is coded in BASIC and asks for the best estimate of the proportion. This it takes to be the modal value m, and from the relationship between the parameters a and b and the mode, i.e. $m = (a-1)/(a+b-2)$, appropriate values of $b = (a(1-m) + 2m-1)/m$ are found. The other input needed is a 50% betting interval around the best estimate.

The program then starts with a β distribution of $a = 1$ and $b = 1$ and by numerical integration checks whether the area inside the 50% betting interval equals the area outside the range. If it does not, then it increments the parameter a by 1, calculating the next b by the relationship $b = (a(1-m) + 2m-1)/m$, and checks the area again. It continues in this fashion, searching through combinations of the parameters a and b until the conditions are satisfied. Quantifying prior judgement about a proportion reduces to providing three values but, unlike the fractile assessment procedure, the mode rather than the median is used.

Asking oneself which is the most likely value (the mode) is probably easier than trying to assess which value exactly splits one's judgement as being as likely as not to be exceeded (the median).

The routine does not work when, as can frequently occur in well-run aspects of accounting systems, the auditor's judgement is that the most likely error rate is zero. When the mode m is zero, it is apparent that the relationship $b = (a(1-m)+2m-1)/m$ does not hold. However, the problem of finding the parameters of a suitable β distribution prior in this case simplifies, and allows an analytical solution. The result is one that we return to in Section 5.4 when we discuss acceptance sampling for compliance testing.

If the mode is zero then

$$0 = (a - 1)/(a + b - 2)$$

from which it follows that $a = 1$. Thus all the β distributions with a mode at zero have the parameter $a = 1$. Figure 4.6 shows a set of such β distributions. The choice of a β distribution with a mode of zero simplifies to a choice of a value for the second parameter b. The formula for the β distribution when $a = 1$ also simplifies to $f(p) \propto (1 - p)^{b-1}$.

The area under this distribution can be found by straight-forward integration. Thus the constant of proportionality

$$1/k = \int_0^1 (1 - p)^{b-1} \, \mathrm{d}p$$

$$1/k = \left[-\frac{1}{b}(1 - p)^b \right]_0^1$$

whence $k = b$.

The area under a β distribution ($a = 1$, $b = b$) between 0 and some value x ($0 < x < 1$) is

$$k \int_0^x f(p) \, \mathrm{d}p = \int_0^x b(1 - p)^{b-1} \, \mathrm{d}p$$

$$= [-(1 - p)^b]_0^x = 1-(1 - x)^b$$

For an application of this result we require the auditor to provide a fractile of his subjective prior. Suppose the most likely error rate is zero, but there could be a small chance, say 5%, that the error rate is greater than one in ten. Equivalently, there is a 95% chance that the proportion is less than 0.1. The β to model such beliefs has $a = 1$, as we know. Knowing $x = 0.1$, we obtain b as follows:

$$1 - (1 - 0.1)^b = 0.95$$
$$(0.9)^b = 0.05$$

Thus

$$b = \log (0.05)/\log (0.9)$$
$$= 28$$

A prior judgement of most likely no errors, but a 95% chance that the error rate is less than 10% is quantified as being the same as having observed no errors in an equivalent prior sample of 28.

```
10 CLS
20 REM A programme for estimating the parameters (a,b) for
30 REM a beta distribution, for modelling prior beliefs
40 REM about a proportion.
50 INPUT "What is your best estimate of the proportion? e.g. 0.52 ":M
60 PRINT""
70 PRINT "Now consider a 50% confidence interval around your best
   estimate. It need not be symmetrical, i.e. plus or minus the same
   amount. Decide on a lower bound and then an upper bound to the
   range"
80 PRINT""
90 PRINT "To remind you, a 50% interval is one in which you bet that
   half the time the true proportion lies. You should have no preference
   to betting that the true proportion lies outside your range, or inside
   your range."
100 PRINT""
110 INPUT"lower bound e.g. 0.3 ",L
120 INPUT"upper bound e.g. 0.55",U
130 A=1
140 REM uses result that the mode for a beta distribution m =
    (a−1)/(a+b−2)
150 B=A*(1−M)/M+2−1/M
160 LSUM=0;MSUM=0:USUM=0
170 REM calculates the area under the beta between 0 and lower
    bound
180 REM the numerical integration is based on Simpsons Rule, however
190 REM since the relative areas only are required, constant terms
    such as the width of the interval, and the constant of proportionality
    are omitted.
200 FOR P = 0 TO L STEP .001
210 LSUM=LSUM+ (P^A)*((1−P)^B)
220 NEXT P
230 REM Now calculates the area inside the range of the lower and
    upper bounds
240 FOR P = L TO U STEP .001
250 MSUM=MSUM+ (P^A)*((1−P)^B)
260 NEXT P
270 REM Finally calculates the area between the upper bound and 1
280 FOR P = U TO 1 STEP .001
290 USUM=USUM+ (P^A)*((1−P)^B)
300 NEXT P
310 REM When the parameters a and b are correct(ish), the area inside
    the range should equal the area outside the range.
```

Figure 4.10. A program for finding a β distribution based on the mode
and the upper and lower quartiles.

```
320  PRINT"iterating...the area inside the range is ";100*MSUM/
     (LSUM+USUM);"%"," of the area outside the range, with a="
     ;A+1;"b="B+1
330  IF MSUM/(LSUM+USUM) > 1 THEN 380
340  REM If the test fails then increase the parameters.
350  A=A+1:IF A=40 THEN 420 ELSE 150
360  REM ends if cannot fit under a=40
370  REM parameters a,b used in the iteration need increasing by 1
380  PRINT""
390  PRINT"The beta function that best approximates your judgement,
     has parameters"

400  PRINT"a,b",A+1,B+1
410  END
420  PRINT"a exceeds 40, so a default is to stop the search. If you want
     to try for a beta with a parameter greater than 40 list line 90 A=1,
     change to A=40. Also change line 350 to A=A+1:IF A=100 then
     500 else 150. Re-run the programme"
```

Figure 4.10. *continued.*

When the modal error rate is zero, and there is a $y\%$ chance that the error rate does not exceed some proportion $x\%$ then $a = 1$ and the parameter b can be found using

$$b = \log(y/100)/\log(1-x/100)$$

This simple result obtains because the integration to find the area under the β distribution is simple. For values of $a > 1$ and $b > 1$ the integration has to be performed by parts.

The alternative to remembering high-school calculus is to use a numerical routine. Figure 4.11 lists a BASIC program that approximates the judgement weight between any range of values for any β distribution.

Using the routine, the connection between the equivalent prior sample and prior judgement weights can be readily explored. For illustration, suppose an auditor has quantified his prior judgement and chosen a β distribution with $a = 2$ and $b = 50$ as the appropriate model. This is equivalent to a prior sample of size 52, with two errors observed. To explore what this model implies about the chance of error rates would be useful for checking the consistency of the model, and would represent a sort of

```
10 CLS
20 PRINT"This routine calculates the area under a beta distribution"
30 PRINT"f(p)=k*(p^(a-1))*((1-p)^(b-1)) with parameters a,b
40 PRINT"used for modelling judgements about a proportion"
50 PRINT""
60 PRINT""
70 INPUT "parameters a,b e.g. 2,6 ",A,B
80 PRINT""
90 PRINT"To evaluate how much judgement weight attatches to any
   range"
100 INPUT"what is the lower end of the range? e.g. 0 ",L
110 INPUT"what is the upper end of the range? e.g. 0.7 ",H
120 LSUM=0:MSUM=0:USUM=0
130 A=A-1:B=B-1
140 FOR P = 0 TO L STEP .0005
150 LSUM=LSUM+(P^A)*((1-P)^B)
160 NEXT P
170 FOR P = L TO H STEP .0005
180 MSUM=MSUM+(P^A)*((1-P)^B)
190 NEXT P
200 FOR P = H TO 1 STEP .0005
210 USUM=USUM+(P^A)*((1-P)^B)
220 NEXT P
230 X=MSUM/(LSUM+USUM)
240 PROB=X/(1+X)
245 PRINT""
246 PRINT""
250 PRINT"Judgement weight between ";L;" and ";H;" for a beta
    distribution"
260 Print"with parameters a= ";A+1;" and b= ";B+1
270 PRINT"                                   ";PROB*100;"%"
```

Figure 4.11. A program for approximating the judgement value between any range of values for any β distribution.

triangulation exercise. To compute the judgement weight to attach to the error rate being under 5%, the parameters 2 and 50 are input in response to line 70 of the routine. The value of 0 in input for the lower end of the range in response to line 100, and the value 0.05 in response to line 110, being the upper end of the range. After a pause the judgement weight of 72% is returned. This calculation can be checked analytically by evaluating

$$k \int_0^{0.05} p\,(1-p)^{49}\mathrm{d}p$$

where

$$k = \frac{(a+b-1)!}{(a-1)!(b-1)} = \frac{51!}{1!\,49!} = 51 \times 50$$

Integrating by parts gives a re-expression of the integral as

$$51 \times 50 \left[-\frac{1}{50} p\,(1-p)^{50} \right]_0^{0.05} + 51 \times 50 \int_0^{0.05} \frac{1}{50}(1-p)^{50}\,\mathrm{d}p$$

$$= \quad -51\,(0.05)\,(0.95)^{50}$$

$$+ \quad [-(1-p)^{51}]_0^{0.05}$$

$$= \quad 0.19621 - (0.95)^{51} + 1$$

$$= \quad 0.73069$$

The numerical routine provides a reasonable approximation.

In this illustration, the auditor has generated an additional non-intuitive 'fact', namely an equivalent prior sample of 50 tested items, where one item in error corresponds to a 73% judgement weight that the error rate in the population is under 5%. The judgement weights that an error rate is under 5%, which corresponds to a variety of equivalent prior samples, are given in Table 4.7. Each entry in this table was computed in the manner of the illustration we have just worked through.

The equivalent prior sample, we have argued, is a useful concept in the problem of quantifying the auditor's subjective beliefs prior to collecting evidence. It means that direct test data can be combined with the indirect evidence that the auditor is steadily accumulating with his growing experience of the accounting systems under review. Whilst the data in Table 4.7 are given in terms of equivalent *prior* samples, it should be noted that these may also be considered to be *posterior* samples. In the sense we have already discussed, a β distribution with $a = 2$ and $b = 50$ may be considered to be the result of a β distribution ($a = 1$, $b = 1$) combined with a sample ($n = 50$, $x = 1$). However, such an equivalent prior sample may also be the result of an

Table 4.7. The probability that an error rate is under 5% corresponding to various equivalent prior samples.

Equivalent prior sample size	Probability (%)		
	Zero equivalent errors in prior sample	One equivalent error in prior sample	Two equivalent errors in prior sample
10	40	10	2
20	63	28	9
30	77	46	21
40	85	61	34
50	90	72	48
60	92	81	60
70	94	87	70
80	94.6	91	78
90	94.7	94	84
100	94.8	96	88

indifference prior $(1,1)$, combined with a sample $(n=20, x=0)$ to which were added further test results $(n=30, x=1)$. The model for combining judgement and evidence treats quantified judgement and quantified evidence symmetrically. There are thus several routes to the same equivalent prior sample. In Table 4.7 an equivalent prior sample of two errors in a sample of size 50 could represent an initial start point, giving a 48% chance that the error rate is under 5%. Again it could represent an indifference prior combined with testing a sample of size[50] and finding two errors. On the other hand, it could represent (i) an initial start point of an equivalent prior sample of zero errors in a sample of size 10, giving a 40% chance of an error rate under 5%; followed by (ii) testing a sample of size 30 and finding one error, raising this judgement weight to 61%; followed by (iii) testing a further sample of size 10, finding a further error and the judgement weight being revised downwards to 48%. It is worthwhile considering the data in Table 4.7 further since they illustrate several features of a formal model for audit judgement.

The manner in which sequential evidence is evaluated is particularly noteworthy. The treatment of quantified prior judgement as an equivalent prior sample, which can be dealt with in exactly the same manner as sample evidence, leads to judgement being based on a process of accumulation of evidence. In the audit process, judgement is steadily refined as the gathering of evidence proceeds. Examining what happens to the mean and variance of a β distribution as it is successively revised to incorporate sample evidence is an idealization of this process. To illustrate this point we consider the evaluation of two samples: the first of size n_2 containing x_2 errors; and the second of size n_3 containing x_3 errors. We take our prior β distribution with parameters a and b, then the prior mean proportion $m_1 = a/(a+b)$. Because we postulate an indifference prior $a=1$, $b=1$, then the prior equivalent sample size is $n_1 = (a+b-2)$ of which $x_1 = (a-1)$ have the characteristic. Representing the prior mean in terms of this equivalent prior sample size $m_1 = (x_1+1)/(n_1+2)$. Apart from the adjustment of 1 and 2 to x_1 and n_1, due to the indifference prior having the parameters $a=1$ and $b=1$, the prior mean is the ratio of the number of errors to sample size. (Strictly the ratio x_1/n_1 is the mode, which corresponds to the maximum likelihood estimator of the error proportion.)

The prior variance, which is $ab/(a+b)^2(a+b+1)$, can be re-expressed in terms of the prior mean, and the prior sample size as $m_1(1-m_1)/(n_1+3)$. It can be readily seen from this re-expression that greater confidence in prior judgement, represented by a larger equivalent prior sample size n_1, results in a smaller variance. The size of the variance is an index of the residual uncertainty in judgement. A certain judgement corresponds to a zero variance, or an equivalent sample size so large as to represent perfect knowledge. An independent third-party certification of an account item, for example, would represent for the auditor a very large sample size because of the reduction in uncertainty of judgement. One could conceive of a taxonomy of the variety of types of audit evidence graded by equivalent sample size. For example, Gray and Munson[21] present the following scheme on the grading of audit evidence:

(i)   The existence of physical objects confirmed by the auditor himself is very good evidence.

(ii)   Analysis carried out by the auditor is good evidence.

(iii) Evidence from independent third parties is good evidence.

(iv) Evidence from third parties in the hands of the company

is good evidence, but may have been manipulated by
management.

(v)   Evidence created in the normal course of business is better
than evidence specially created to satisfy the auditor.

(vi) The best informed source of audit evidence will normally
be the management of the company subject to audit, but
management's lack of independence reduces its value as
a source of such evidence.

(vii) Written evidence is of greater value to the auditor than
oral evidence.

(viii) Properly established and tested systems of control enhance
the reliability of evidence derived from them.

(ix) Good evidence about the future is particularly difficult to
obtain and is less reliable than evidence about past
events.

(x)   Evidence may be upgraded by the skilful use of corroborative evidence.

On this last item the up-grading of evidence by the skilful use
of corroborative evidence is really the up-grading of *judgement*
by the sequential evaluation of evidence. The changing mean and
variance of our β model of judgement demonstrates this effect

Table 4.8. The change in the mean and variance for two sequential
samples (x_2,n_2) and (x_3,n_3).

Sample	Mean	Variance
Prior	$m_1=(x_1+1)/(n_1+2)$	$m_1(1-m_1)/(n_1+3)$
First	$m_2+(x_1+x_2+1)/(n_1+n_2+2)$	$m_2(1-m_2)/(n_1+n_2+3)$
	or	
	$m_2 = \dfrac{x_2}{n_2} + w_2\left(m_1 - \dfrac{x_2}{n_2}\right)$	
	where $w_2=(n+2)/(2+n_1+n_2)$	
Second	$m_3=(x_1+x_2+x_3+1)/(n_1+n_2+n_3+2)$	$m_3(1-m_3)/(n_1+n_2+n_3+3)$
	or	
	$m_3 = \dfrac{x_3}{n_3} + w_3\left(m_2 - \dfrac{x_3}{n_3}\right)$	
	where	
	$w_3=(n_1+n_2+2)/(n_1+n_2+n_3+2)$	

for sequential samples (x_2, n_2) and (x_3, n_3) and can be tabulated as shown in Table 4.8. The revised mean after the first sample is a mixture of the sample proportion (x_2/n_2) and the prior mean m_1. In this tabulation the revision of the mean is expressed in terms of an error correction. If the difference between the sample mean and the prior mean is small, there is little adjustment to the sample result. If the sample result is unexpected in terms of its departure from the prior mean, there is a larger adjustment of the result towards the prior mean $(m_1 - x_2/n_2)$. The coefficient for the error adjustment (w_2) depends on the equivalent prior sample size n_1 and the sample size of n_2. If n_1 is small compared with n_2, then this adjustment of the sample result towards the prior mean will also be small. More weight will be given to the actual sample and less to the hypothetical sample. In terms of the variance, we saw that a larger n_1 implies smaller variance and hence greater confidence. The effect of the first sample (n_2) on confidence is in the same direction as the effect of the second sample. As the sequential samples accumulate, so the variance falls. The sequential revision of judgement results in smaller and smaller uncertainty. Once prior judgement is conceived of as being equivalent to a prior sample, we have a logical basis not just for quantifying prior judgement, but also for incorporating sample evidence with prior beliefs, and understanding the audit evidence gathering process as it proceeds.

4.8 Summary

In this chapter we have discussed some important ideas for implementing the formal model of audit judgement. Although we have concerned ourselves exclusively with the problem of forming an opinion about a proportion we have met most of the key ideas:

(i)   conjugate distributions as a standard way of quantifying judgements;

(ii) use of Bayes' theorem as the method of combining the likelihood of audit evidence with the quantified judgements;

(iii) the indifference, ignorance, or diffuse prior to represent the situation in which no weight is to be given to prior judgements; and

(iv) representing non-sampling and prior judgement as being equivalent to a hypothetical sample.

These same ideas are used when considering the problem of judgements about balances. Our formal model behaves intuitively, balancing evidence and judgement. The computations can, however, be tedious when performed by hand. Implementation in the field does require computing. An interactive conversational program can also embed the expert knowledge needed to take a practitioner step by step through the evaluation of audit evidence to a defensible opinion. The ability to view prior judgement as equivalent to already having tested a sample is the key to the cost advantages which the implementation of this approach promises. The conventional approach to applying statistics in audit contexts confines itself to the sort of methods which require only comparatively simple tables to execute. The simplification is achieved by using approximations which require taking very large and uneconomic sample sizes. If one takes very large samples then, as we saw, the effect of prior judgements is much diminished, which is one reason why ignoring such effects in the conventional approach is a legitimate approximation. However, audit evidence to support an opinion can be very expensive to collect, which is why throwing away data implicit in prior judgements does not make sense. We now have the technology to make such an approach work. Having examined the risk estimation issues involved in proportions or attribute sampling, we need to see what is involved in implementing this approach for substantive test purposes or estimating the magnitude of the monetary error in accounting population. However, before tackling this important extension, there are some details about risk evaluation which we have not addressed. These details are dealt with in the following chapter.

Notes and references

1 The first explicit discussion can be found in K.H. Kraft (1968) Statistical sampling for auditors: a new look, *The Journal of Accounting*, **Aug.**, 49–56.

2 In a recent test Abdolmohammadi demonstrated in an experiment, involving 138 practising auditors from seven different firms, that quantifying judgement gives a significant efficiency advantage. See: M.J. Abdolmohammadi (1986) Efficiency of the Bayesian approach in compliance testing: some empirical evidence, *Auditing: A Journal of Practice and Theory*, **5** (2), 1–16.

3 For a useful source to the field of quantifying judgement, see: C.S. Spelzler and C.A.S. Stack von Holstein (1975) Probability encoding in decision analysis, *Management Science*, **22** (3), 341–358.

4 A good summary of previous research is given in: I. Solomon, L.A. Tomassini, M.B. Romney and J.L. Krogstad (1984) Probability elicitation in auditing: additional evidence on the equivalent prior sample, *Advances in Accounting*, **1**, 267–290.

5 Experiments demonstrating the over-confidence of estimators are described in: P.G. Moore (1983) *The Business of Risk*, p. 50 ff. Cambridge: Cambridge University Press.

6 The behavioural research on the way complex judgements are reduced to manageable proportions has been reviewed by D. Gwilliam in *A Survey of Auditing Research* (1987), Chapter 13. London: Prentice Hall.

7 Further details of the CADA package, and of other software for Bayesian methods in statistical auditing are given in the appendix to Chapter 7.

8 Eight methods of quantifying judgement, of which four have been tested explicitly in an audit decision context, are described in: M.J. Abdolmohammadi (1985) Bayesian inference research in auditing: some methodological suggestions, *Contemporary Accounting Research*, **2**, 76–94.

9 One of the first studies to test the feasibility of the equivalent prior sample (EQPS) in an audit context is that by W.L. Felix (1976) Evidence on alternative means of assessing prior probability distributions for audit decision making, *The Accounting Review*, **Oct.**, 800–807. Felix reported that his subject found the method had intuitive appeal, and it seemed that the difficulties which remained could be solved through training. Subsequent studies have been more equivocal in supporting EQPS—see: M.J. Abdolmohammadi (1985) Bayesian inference in substantive testing: an ease of use criterion, *Advances in Accounting*, **2**, 275–289; M.A. Crosby (1981) Bayesian statistics in auditing: a comparision of probability elicitation techniques, *The Accounting Review*, **Apr.**, 355–365.

10 T.W. McRae (1974) *Statistical Sampling for Audit and Control*. London: John Wiley & Sons.

11 If the probability of an error is p, then the probability of no error is $(1 - p)$. The probability of a series of n without error is $(1 - p) \times (1 - p) \times (1 - p) \times \ldots \times (1 - p) = (1 - p)^n$.

In general, the probability of x errors in a sample of size n independently drawn items, with a constant probability for a single error p is given by the binomial distribution

$$\text{prob}\,(x,n\mid p) = \frac{n!}{x!\,(n-x)!}\,p^{x}(1-p)^{n-x}$$

For further details see, for example, M. Hamburg (1983) *Statistical Analysis for Decision Making*, 3rd edn. New York: Harcourt Brace Jovanovich.

12 Bayes' theorem is a basic result in elementary probability theory the derivation of which can be found in a number of texts, see, for example, Hamburg p. 75 (see note 11).

13 The unconditional probability $P(Z)$ is the a constant of proportionality. That is if $P(Z) = c^{-1}$, then $P(A|Z) = c\,P(A) \times P(Z|A)$. Now if there are n states A_i ($i=1$ to n), the posterior judgement weights for each state when summed across every state must total 1 in order to be coherent. That is

$$\sum_{i=1}^{n} P(A_i|Z) = \sum_{i=1}^{n} cP(A_i) \times P(Z|A_i) = 1$$

from which we deduce that

$$c^{-1} = \sum_{i=1}^{n} P(A_i) \times P(Z|A_i) = P(Z)$$

The rescaling constant c is thus calculated by forming the sum for every state of the product of the prior judgement weight for each state with the likelihood of observing the signal in that state.

14 That is $x = 1$ success in $n = 10$ trials of a binomial process using the equation given in footnote 12.

15 See, for example, W.A. Watson, T. Philipson and P.J. Oates (1981) *Numerical Analysis: The Mathematics of Computing*, 2nd edn, Chap. 9. London: Edward Arnold. Using Simpson's rule the interval $(0,1)$ is divided into small graduations of width h, e.g. $h = 0.001$, to give $1/h$ points at which $f(p)$ is calculated. The area under the curve is then

$$h\left(\sum_{i=1}^{1/h-1} f(ih) + 0.5f(0) + 0.5f(1) \right).$$

This is simple to program. The graphs in this chapter were prepared using Lotus 123 and this approximation.

16 J.W. Pratt, H. Raiffa and R. Schaifer (1965) *Introduction to Statistical Decision Theory*. New York: McGraw-Hill. These authors suggest a fractile assessment procedure. E. Blocher (1981) Assessment of prior distributions: the effect on required sample size in Bayesian audit sampling, *Accounting and Business Research*, **12** (45), 11–20, uses a method which requires the mean and variance, as discussed in the text.

17   From: M.R. Novick and P.H. Jackson (1974) *Statistical Methods for Educational and Psychological Research*. New York: McGraw-Hill.
18   E. Blocher and J.C. Robertson (1976) 'Bayesian sampling procedures for auditors: computer assisted instruction', *The Accounting Review*, **Apr.**, 359–363.
19   See note 16.
20   See Novick and Jackson, pp. 167–170 (see note 17).
21   I. Gray and S. Manson (1989) *The Audit Process: Principles, Practice and Cases*, pp. 90–94. New York: Van Nostrand Reinhold.

Chapter 5

Implementation and Balancing Risks

5.1 Materiality

This chapter much more than the previous ones suffers from the infancy of systematic empirical audit research. The analysis is that much further away from specific quantitative guidelines. The crucial questions of how materiality limits should be set, what the tolerable levels of audit risk are, and how large the sample collected should be, depend on balancing costs for which we do not have good estimates. Materiality as an idea does not really derive from auditing, although it has great significance to auditors. Materiality comes from the users of financial information. It is essentially an accounting concept relating the threshold amount of omission or misstatement in an account item that would influence some user's decision. Users and uses of financial statements are diverse, the auditor has to imagine the stereotypical user and context which the courts might have in mind if it ever came to it. This will vary from context to context.

Although the problem of defining justifiable materiality limits precisely appears intractable, that is not to say that there has not been some outstanding research done in this area.[1] Steinbart[2] has published details about AUDITPLANNER, a program which interrogates an auditor about a client, and uses a set of expert rules to set the materiality level for audit planning purposes. The expert rules developed are not based on empirical evidence or research, but 'the wisdom of practice', the guidelines that the expert has learnt over the years as conventional.

The data and rules came from working closely with a single audit partner and formalizing the judgement model which he used on actual engagements. Some 95 rules were used in the prototype. An illustration of a sample session with AUDITPLANNER is given in the Appendix to this chapter. The general strategy adopted is illustrated in Figure 5.1. There are three subdecisions involved:

   (i)   choosing the basis for calculating materiality (for example the income from continuing operations, or the average income from the previous 3 years, or the amount of owner's equity, or for a financial institution the income from continuing operation divided by the average rate of return on the portfolio);

  (ii)   choosing a percentage rate to apply to the materiality base; and

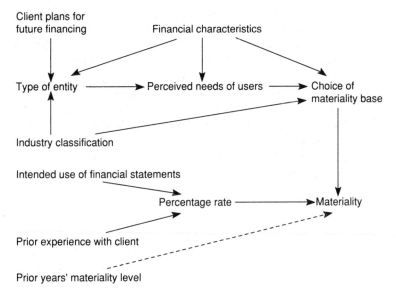

Figure 5.1. AUDITPLANNER strategy.[3]

(iii) the actual calculation.

The choice of materiality basis depends on whether the principal users are assumed to be primarily interested in financial position and solvency, or primarily interested in the results of current operations. The exact choice of the percentage rate in special situations was not published because of the sensitive nature of such decisions. However, the default rate was set as follows. If:

(i)   the financial statements are not going to be used in connection with a public offering of the clients securities;
(ii)   the financial statements are not going to be used in connection with a transfer of interests in the client;
(iii) the financial statements are not going to be used in connection with a contest for the control of the client;
(iv)   the financial statements are not going to be used to settle some outstanding litigation in which the client is involved;
(v)   the financial statements are not going to be used in connection with an inquiry by a regulatory agency; and
(vi)   the client is not in violation of, and is not likely to be found to be in violation of, restrictive debt covenants relating to the results of continuing operations;

then a percentage rate of 5% should be used to calculate materiality.

When AUDITPLANNER was tested with six of the partner's colleagues some lack of consensus was indicated, the prototype almost always recommended a materiality level that was lower than that previously selected on clients. One auditor said that he would approach materiality judgement in a wholly different way, only three said that they would accept the expert system's recommendation. However, all six would want to use AUDIT-PLANNER as a decision aid and, with only one exception, would permit subordinates to use the package as a decision aid, and as a training device. This is an exciting application of artificial intelligence. As more such systems are built, the research agenda of teaching automata to replicate expert judgement will lead to new insights, understanding and the ability to articulate how to make such judgements.

5.2 Loss functions

An unresolved question from our example in the previous chapter is: What would be a true and fair view of the bad debt provision? Imagine the situation if an auditor had to come up with a single number rather than a range of acceptable values. Which single number would best summarize the situation? In order to decide something is 'best' we need some criteria to judge by. We need to know what it costs us to be wrong. How the costs vary with the size of error is known as the loss function.

Loss functions are a convenient abstraction in a number of applications. For example, in drawing a line of best fit through a scatterplot of points, a conventional criterion is to minimize the sum of the squared errors to give the ordinary least squares fit. In Magistrates' Courts, the sentencing guidelines roughly increase the fine for speeding for every mile per hour by which the speed limit is exceeded. For simplicity of exposition, we model the loss function for the true and fair view point estimate as in the classic newsboy problem.[4] The newsboy problem is a famous question in management science, in which the seller of a perishable commodity has to decide on the optimal quantity of stock to order before knowing the demand for the day. If too little is ordered the seller loses profit on the unfilled demand. If too much stock is ordered the seller loses profit on the cost of the date-expired excess stock. Like the newsboy ordering tomorrow's papers, the auditor has to form a view on a true and fair amount, in advance of knowing that a court might subsequently decide that the amount is too little or too much. The cost consequences of an over- or under-estimation might be different. (As noted in Chapter 2 from their analysis of court cases, St Pierre and Anderson[5] did not find a single case concerned with excessive conservatism, which suggests that we should consider asymmetrical loss functions.)

Let us denote the unknown amount that a court might decide as true and fair as x. The auditor will have a formed view as to the range of values this might take, and his judgement will be described by a posterior probability density judgement weight function $f(x)$. The auditor must choose some value x^* as the single point value to represent the true and fair balance. If the

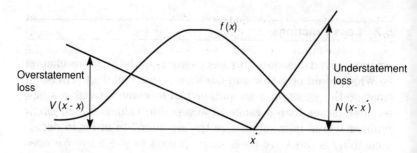

Figure 5.2. Loss function for the bad debt provision.

auditor under-estimates then the cost penalty will be at some rate N, multiplied by the amount of understatement. If the auditor over-estimates the provision, then the cost of being excessively prudent will be at some different rate V times the amount of overstatement. The way we have set the problem up can be represented as shown in Figure 5.2, where $f(x)$ is the judgement weight function on x the size of the provision, and x^* is the true and fair value of x. If $x^* < x$ the loss is $N(x-x^*)$. If $x^* > x$ the loss is $V(x^*-x)$.

The loss function has been formulated in quite a particular way, although the weight function $f(x)$ is quite general. The costs of erring either way, N and V, can take any amount. The choice of the best point for a true and fair value x^*, is one which minimizes the expected loss.

It can be shown[6] that the best value of x^* is given by the $N/(V+N)$th fractile of $f(x)$. If the auditor considers that the consequences of understatement are nine times more serious than the consequences of overstatement, then the 90% fractile should be chosen. Again, if the auditor considers that the consequences of over- or under-statement are the same, then the median should be the choice. This is a surprising result. Until one thinks about balancing the costs of over- and under-statement one might have suspected that the mean or the mode of the subjective probability distribution would have been the true and fair value.[7] Although we do not know what values to attach to N and V, we only have to estimate their ratio in order to decide which fractile gives the true and fair view. (If $N = t \times V$, then we need the $t/(1+t) \times 100\%$ fractile.)

Looking back to the question of a true and fair bad debt provision in the previous chapter, the final beliefs were expressed as a β distribution ($a = 3$, $b = 62$). This has a 75% fractile at the proportion 0.06 and would be the true and fair value if costs of overstatement were three times the costs of understatement. It has a 99% fractile at the proportion 0.12. Were the costs of imprudence to be considered 99 times more than the costs of prudence, then the auditor would settle on a provision based on a proportion of bad debts as high as 0.12.

We do not know what the relative costs of audit error are. We do not know what the shape of the loss function is. Perhaps there is some materiality range, some level of precision in which zero loss is involved and outside which the costs of error increase sharply.

In general, without knowing the loss functions it is not possible to give a specific quantitative answer to the point value problem. In the absence of detailed data about more complex loss functions, the linear approximation is, as in the newsboy problem, a practical choice, particularly since it leads to a simple recommendation.

5.3 Optimal sample sizes

Loss functions are also needed in deciding the appropriate amount of audit evidence to collect. In Chapter 3 we glossed over what constitutes sufficient massing of judgement weights, as well as the exact process by which prior judgements get 'massed' by evidence. We subsequently tackled the second of these issues but not the first. In order to model the sufficiency of evidence issue in a general way we need four components:

(i) a loss function for the errors of over- or under-statement (in general we denote this by $l(x)$)

(ii) a conjugate prior to represent the non-sampling evidence ($f(x)$);

(iii) a likelihood function for the sample evidence (this will depend on the sample size n, so we represent it as a function $L(n)$); and

(iv) a cost structure for audit sampling (this may have a fixed component, F, as well as a variable cost, V, for each item tested. This is represented as $F + Vn$.).

Table 5.1. Factors that influence the substantive test sample size.

Factor	Conditions leading to:	
	Smaller sample size	Larger sample size
Inherent risk	Lower inherent risk	Higher inherent risk
Reliance on internal control	Higher reliance on internal control	Lower reliance on internal control
Reliance on other substantive tests related to same audit objective and class of transactions	Substantial reliance to be placed on other substantive tests	Little or no reliance to be placed on other substantive tests
Measure of tolerable error for a specific audit objective	Larger measure of tolerable error	Smaller measure of tolerable error
Expected size and frequency of errors	Smaller errors or lower frequency	Larger errors or higher frequency
Population value	Smaller monetary significance to the financial information	Larger monetary significance to the financial information
Number of items in population	Normally no significant effect on sample size (unless the population is very small)	
Overall assurance required	Lower overall assurance	Higher overall assurance
Stratification	Stratification of the population	No stratification of the population

Table 5.2. Factors that influence the compliance test sample size.

Factor	Conditions leading to:	
	Smaller sample size	Larger sample size
Planned reliance on internal control*	Lower reliance on internal control	Higher reliance on internal control
Maximum rate of deviation (tolerable error)	Potentially higher rate of deviation for planned reliance on internal control	Potentially lower rate of deviation for planned reliance on internal control
Allowable risk of over-reliance	Higher risk of over-reliance on internal control	Lower risk of over-reliance on internal control
Likely rate of population deviation†	Lower expected rate of deviation in population	Higher expected rate of deviation in population
Number of items in population	Normally no significant affect on sample size (unless the population is very small)	

* Compliance tests are normally not necessary when no reliance is placed on internal controls.
† Larger samples are necessary when deviations occur, in order to obtain more precise conclusions. However, high expected deviation rates normally warrant little, if any, reliance on internal controls and, in such a case, compliance testing should be omitted.

The optimal size of sample n is the one which minimizes the following expression:

$$(F+Vn) + \int_{-\infty}^{+\infty} l(x)\,f(x)\,L(n)\,\mathrm{d}x$$

The integral gives the expected cost of error, which falls with increasing sample size as the prior judgement becomes 'massed' by the weight of evidence. The term Vn increases as the sample size increases. The optimal sample size is achieved when the cost of a single extra test item, V, is greater than the expected reduction in the loss from over- or under-statement.

In general, the optimal number of items to test must be found iteratively, by increasing the sample size until the minimum cost is reached. The calculation is tedious, and is again something best left to a computer.[8] We can, however, make some *ceteris paribus* observations about optimal sample sizes:

(i)   The less serious the consequences of over- or under-statement, $l(x)$, the smaller the size of sample should be taken. In particular the wider the acceptable precision or materiality interval the smaller the sample. The overall assurance required, the measure of tolerable error for a specific audit objective, the inherent risk are all related to the loss function.

(ii) The stronger the prior judgements, $f(x)$, the smaller the size of sample. Strong priors can be due to reliance on internal control and to reliance on related substantive tests.

(iii) The more expensive the variable cost of testing, V, the smaller the sample size.

(iv) As far as likelihoods are concerned, the position is slightly more involved, to make generalizations one needs to predict what the evidence is going to be, because likelihood is a function of the data. In general, it is not the size of the anticipated errors that is important, but their distribution. Errors of varying sizes make it more difficult to resolve uncertainty about the average size of error.

The auditing guideline on audit sampling[9] gives in two tables (which are reproduced as Tables 5.1 and 5.2) its own summary of the main factors influencing sample size. Curiously the cost of sampling is not mentioned.

In the current audit environment in which audit sample sizes are set more by tradition than logic, playing with a formal computerized model serves as an important training to professional judgement. For instance, it is possible to devise situations in which zero is the optimal sample size! When non-sampling prior judgement is strong, the costs of error are low, the materiality range is wide and the expense of sampling high, a defensible opinion could rest entirely on the quantified conjugate prior. To say more about optimal sample sizes requires specific assumptions to be made about the four components in order to simplify the decision context.

5.4 Acceptance sampling for compliance testing

We conclude by looking at the Bayesian approach to acceptance sampling discussed by Blocher.[10] Acceptance sampling involves a simple audit decision context. An auditor has to check the attributes of a particular accounting population, or accounting system and decide whether the error rate is small enough for it to be considered acceptable or reliable. In this application the general loss function is considered to take a form which allows for it to be operationalized by merely requiring identification of a maximum acceptable error rate, and a maximum probability of exceeding this rate. This latter risk is known as the reliability of the test.

It is a simplification which is important in monetary unit sampling, in which the loss function is reduced to merely requiring a monetary precision and an associated reliability factor. It is left as an exercise to the reader to deduce what simplifications are needed for a loss function to be represented in this way.

For illustration, an auditor may decide that a situation is acceptable if the error rate is less than the maximum of 6%. The auditor is prepared to tolerate a risk of 1 in 20 that he might incorrectly accept the population. This 5% risk level is the desired test reliability. Now let us consider the situation if the auditor has prior beliefs about the error proportion, and needs to decide

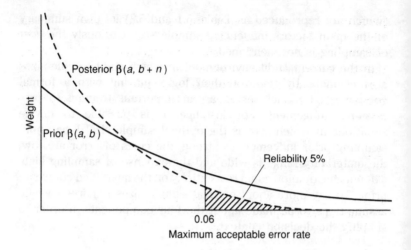

Figure 5.3. Bayesian acceptance sampling.

the smallest size of sample which should be taken (assuming that there are no errors)? The problem may be depicted as shown in Figure 5.3. The problem reduces to finding a posterior distribution for which the 95% fractile is 0.06.

Suppose further that the auditor formed a view on the basis of his past experience that there were most likely zero errors; however, if there were errors then the average rate was about 4%. Now the mode of zero suggests a parameter $a = 1$ for the prior β distribution which models these beliefs (i.e. $0 = (a-1)/(a+b-2)$. A mean of 0.04 in turn suggests a value of $b = 24$ (i.e. $0.04 = a/(b+a)$). (The reasonableness of this prior could be checked by feeding back to the auditor for example that such a β distribution gives an inherent risk of an error rate over 0.10 of 6.5%). A β distribution prior ($a=1$, $b=24$) is equivalent to having already tested a sample of size 23 without error. Now a β distribution posterior with $a = 1$ and $b = 43$ has a 95% fractile at 0.06. Consequently, the size of sample, n, assuming $x = 0$, is $43 - 24 = 19$ items.

If the auditor was unwilling to quantify his prior beliefs (so implicitly $a = 1$ and $b = 1$) a sample of size 42 would be needed with zero errors to achieve the same acceptance criterion. In this illustration, by going to the trouble of quantifying prior judgement, the size of sample for testing has been cut in half. Blocher[10] does point out that this result does depend crucially on the prior. If instead the auditor suspected before sampling that the error rate was in excess of the maximum acceptable, then he would require considerably more evidence to be persuaded to the contrary, than had he stuck with an indifference prior.

Notes and references

1 For a review see: D. Gwilliam (1987) *A Survey of Auditing Research*, Chap. 14. Englewood Cliffs, NJ: Prentice Hall.
2 P.J. Steinbart (1987) Materiality: a case study using expert systems, *The Accounting Review*, **Jan.**, 97–116.
3 From Steinbart (see note 2).
4 Churchman, Ackoff, Arnoff (1957) *Introduction to Operations Research*, pp. 210ff. Chichester: Wiley.
5 K. St Pierre and J.A. Anderson (1984) An analysis of factors associated with lawsuits against public accountants, *Accounting Review*, **Apr.**, 242–263.
6 The expected loss (E(L)) depends on the choice of x^*, as follows:

$$\text{E(L)} = \int_{-\infty}^{x^*} V(x-x^*)f(x)\,\mathrm{d}x + \int_{x^*}^{+\infty} N(x^*-x)f(x)\,\mathrm{d}x$$

The minimum expected loss occurs when $\partial\text{E(L)}/\partial x^* = 0$, i.e. when

$$-V\int_{-\infty}^{x^*} f(x)\,\mathrm{d}x + N\int_{x^*}^{\infty} f(x)\,\mathrm{d}x = 0$$

and

$$-V\int_{-\infty}^{x^*} f(x)\,\mathrm{d}x + N\left(1-\int_{-\infty}^{x^*} f(x)\,\mathrm{d}x\right) = 0$$

So

$$N/(V+N) = \int_{-\infty}^{x^*} f(x)\,\mathrm{d}x$$

7 If the loss function is quadratic, i.e. loss $= (x-x^*)^2$, then the best value to choose is the mean. If the loss function is a step loss, i.e.

$$\text{loss} = \begin{cases} 0 \text{ if } | x - x^* | \leq K \\ L \text{ if } | x - x^* | > K \end{cases}$$

then the best value to choose is the mode.

8   An excellent discussion of this problem is given in: R.L. Winkler
    (1972) *Introduction to Bayesian Inference and Decision*, pp. 348–376.
    New York: Rinehart Winston.

APPENDIX 5.1
A sample session with AUDITPLANNER

This is an example of a session with AUDITPLANNER. Each session
begins with an introductory statement which is followed by a
series of questions. The same sequence of questions would *not*
be asked for all clients, because later questions depend upon
answers given to earlier ones. The capitalized entries that follow
the double asterisks are the user's responses.

You will be asked a series of questions about a client you are
about to audit. On the basis of your answers to those questions,
a set of recommendations will be presented about the appropriate
materiality level(s) to be used in planning the extent of audit
procedures.

1.   What is the name of the client?
**   EXAMPLE

2.   What is Example's main line of business or industry
     classification?
**   MANUFACTURING

3.   Is this the first time that we have audited Example?
**   NO

4.   Have there been any acquisitions which either singly or in
     total amount to ten percent or more of client's total assets?
**   NO

5.   Some of the questions that follow will ask you to input dollar amounts from the client's financial statements. Will your answers be in terms of thousands of dollars?
**   YES

6.   Does Example have any publicly-traded debt or equity securities?
**   YES

7.   What do you project retained earnings to be?
**   7616

8.   What is the amount of current assets?
**   5822

9.   What is the amount of current liabilities?
**   3009

10. What do you estimate the annual income from continuing operations to be?
**   3786

11. Are the financial statements going to be used in connection with public offering of securities?
**   NO

12. Are the financial statements going to be used in connection with a transfer of interests in Example?
**   NO

13. Are the financial statements going to be used in connection with a contest for control of Example?
**   NO

14. Are the financial statements being used to settle some litigation involving Example?
**   NO

15. Are the financial statements being used in connection with an inquiry by a regulatory commission?
**   NO

16. How much long-term debt does Example have?
**   882

17. Does Example have any covenants on either its long-term debt or existing lines-of-credit?
** YES

18. Does Example have any debt covenants which restrict dividends to a percentage of either current earnings or cash flow?
** NO

19. Do any of Example's debt covenants require it to maintain some level of earnings?
** NO

20. Does Example have any debt covenants which require it to use part of its cash flow to retire its debt?
** NO

The overall materiality level to be used in planning the extent of audit procedures is 189 300.

The reasons for the materiality judgement are as follows:

The calculation of the materiality level was based on the use of income-from-continuing-operations as the base for the materiality calculation. The materiality level was calculated using a percentage rate of 0.05.

Example of AUDITPLANNER's explanation capabilities that can be exercised during a consultation session

The following dialogue illustrates how the normal series of questions that AUDITPLANNER asks can be interrupted to find out *why* a particular question was being asked. As before, the capitalized entries following the double asterisks represent the user's responses. The other statements are AUDITPLANNER's responses to the questions.

3. Is this the first time that we have audited Example?
** WHY

[i.e. why is it important to determine whether this is the first time that we have audited Example?]

    [1.0]   Whether this is the first time that we have audited a client is one of the five standard parameters that identify a client. This may be useful later in the consultations. For example, it is relevant in determining whether there is a need to reduce the calculated materiality level due to the increased risk associated with an initial audit of the client and is relevant in determining the percentage rate used to determine the materiality level.

[back to question 3 ...]

** YES

[NOTE: several questions asked by AUDITPLANNER are skipped until the next time the user asks 'WHY'.]

10. Is Example filing with a regulatory agency in preparation for the sale of its securities in a public market?

** WHY

[i.e. *why* is it important to determine whether Example is filing with a regulatory agency in preparation for the sale of its securities in a public market?]

[2.0] This will aid in determining the type of entity that Example is. It has already been established that

[2.1] it is suspected that the type of entity that Example is is private. Therefore, if

[2.2] Example is not filing with a regulatory agency in preparation for the sale of its securities in a public market, and

[2.3] Example does not intend to go public within the next two or three years, then it is definite (1.0) that the type of entity Example is is private. [RULE007]

[NOTE: AUDITPLANNER explains the current rule being followed that causes it to ask question 10 about Example's plans for future financing.]

[back to question 10 ...]

** HOW 2.1

[NOTE: rather than answering the question, the user wants to explore further the line of reasoning being followed by AUDIT-

PLANNER. Here AUDITPLANNER is asked about one of the conclusions that it has already made.]

[i.e. *how* was it established that it is suspected that the type of entity Example is is private?]

> [2.4] RULE056 was used to conclude that the type of entity Example is is private (.). Thus, it has been established that it is suspected that the type of entity Example is is private.

[back to question 10 ...]

** HOW 2.4

[i.e. *how* was RULE056 used?]

It has already been established that

> [4.1] Example does not have any publicly traded debt or equity securities, and
>
> [4.2] Example does not have restrictive debt covenants that are measured by or depend on periodic financial statement amounts or ratios that involve results of operations, and
>
> [4.3] Example is not controlled by a public entity. Therefore there is strongly suggestive evidence (0.9) that the type of entity Example is is private. [RULE056].

Chapter 6

Substantive Testing: Bayes' Mean Difference

6.1 Introduction

In the preceding chapters the main components of a model for coherent audit judgements were described in great detail using the example of a bad debt provision based on a proportion. Forming risk judgements about proportions, particularly very low proportions, is an important problem in auditing. In compliance tests, where the auditor is trying to satisfy himself that the internal controls on which he intends to rely have been operating over all items irrespective of their monetary value, the essence is to form a defensible judgement about the proportion of errors. Proportions by definition lie in the range between zero and one, and in compliance tests items are either correct or incorrect and their value is not important. By contrast, in substantive testing, where the auditor has to form a judgement about the completeness, accuracy and validity of accounting records and financial statements, the amount of money involved is not irrelevant. Money balances can take any amount from the very large and positive to the very large and negative, as can the errors involved. In substantive testing the auditor has to form a defensible judgement about the magnitude of the monetary errors. The general approach to this problem is the same as that described for sampling a proportion.

   (i) Quantify prior judgements on the size of the error—this is equivalent to having already taken a prior sample;
   (ii) collect audit evidence;
   (iii) revise judgement in the light of the evidence about the size and frequency of the errors that have been discovered by combining the prior sample with the actual sample; and
   (iv) balance the costs of evidence against the expected cost of errors, and decide whether the size of error is:
        case A completely within the materiality range of the assertions of management;
        case B substantially within the materiality range;
        case C materially different from managements assertion; or
        case D too uncertain to attest to.

Our general approach has hitherto drawn on standard Bayesian methods which are commonly met in other contexts and are thus discussed in a number of introductory textbooks.

   However, in substantive testing the auditor faces a specialist problem because he is typically faced with the problem of sampling and estimating rare errors. The importance and particular difficulty of this problem in auditing has attracted much academic research and given rise to many proposals within the last decade or so, of which perhaps only monetary unit sampling (MUS) which is discussed in Chapter 7, has so far percolated into textbooks. In this chapter we describe the model proposed by Felix and Grimlund.[1] We first discuss the problem of trying to estimate rare errors using a classical mean difference estimator, before describing the Bayesian approach of Felix and Grimlund.

6.2 Mean difference estimation

The audit task in substantive testing is to form a view of the total error amount embedded in an account balance. A number of papers have reported on the patterns of errors found in accounting populations. Major studies have been conducted by Neter and Loebbecke,[2] Ramage et al.,[3] Johnson et al.,[4] Hylas and Ashton,[5] Ham et al.,[6] and Kreutzfeldt and Wallace.[7] Although there are differences in their findings, common features are that the error rates (the proportion of accounts that are in error) vary significantly but, in the majority of audit situations, the error rate is low. For example, Ramage et al.[3] found that about 60% of the populations had an error rate of under 5%, whilst Johnson et al.[4] found that 75% of sales ledgers had error rates of under 9%. The error rate does not appear to be associated with the size of the errors. That is, just because the frequency of error is low, does not imply anything about the size of individual errors, which can be large or small.

Kaplan[8] comments that: 'an auditing population is actually a mixture of two quite different populations; one consists of a larger number of correct items; the other is the much smaller population of item in errors. Techniques ... which do not explicitly recognise these fundamentally different populations seem inadequate for auditing applications'.

For a simple demonstration of Kaplan's observation consider the performance of the classical mean-difference estimator. When an auditor uses difference estimation, an unrestricted random sample from the population under review is taken and then tested for any differences between the amounts recorded in the books and the audited amounts. The difference can be either an over-estimate (book amount exceeds audited amount) or an under-estimate (audited amount exceeds book amount). The auditor calculates the mean of the sample of differences and then extrapolates the result to provide an estimate of the total error in the population.

If there are many errors in the accounting population and the errors are roughly the same size, then one can form a fairly good estimate of the total error in the whole population in this way. If, however, as is common in well-managed accounting systems, errors are rare, then when a sample is taken there is a strong possibility of finding zero errors. For the auditor who is unwilling to quantify his prior judgement and wishes to support his opinion by this evidence alone, he will have no confidence at all in extrapolating such a sample result of no errors to the whole population. The auditor is in a quandary. Is the whole population error free? How large could the errors that have not been found be? Should he collect more evidence?

In this chapter we argue that for the auditor who has quantified his prior judgements and recognized that he faces a mixture problem can then quite happily cope with such a sample result. Despite observing zero errors in a sample, the auditor will have a defensible basis for his opinion about the size of the errors that have not been found.

6.3   Bayes' mean difference estimator

Audit errors are generated by a mixture of processes. Figures 6.1 and 6.2 show the distribution of errors for two typical audits, taken from the study by Johnson *et al.*[4] Audit 69 was the sales ledger for an auto services business. The total account balance

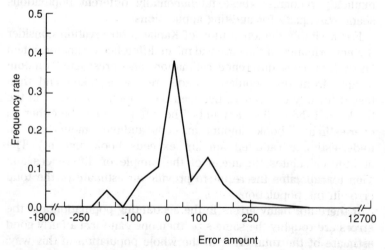

Figure 6.1. Distribution of errors in a typical sales ledger (audit 69[4]).

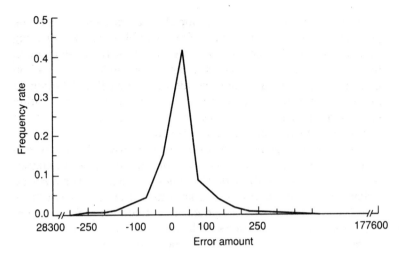

Figure 6.2. Distribution of errors in a typical stock ledger (audit 23⁴).

was \$31.49 million, made up of approximately 19 000 customer accounts. There were errors in 14% of these accounts. Audit 23 was a stock audit for an electrical machinery manufacturer. There were some 31 000 items of stock with a total value of £31.45 million. The error rate was 29%. Johnson and his colleagues demonstrate that this pattern of errors cannot be modelled by a single distribution. It appears that one needs a mixture of at least two.

Such an approach to the problem is discussed in Felix and Grimlund.[1] There are two components needed to formally model audit judgements involved in substantive testing:

  (i) judgements about the proportion of errors in the population irrespective of their magnitude; and
 (ii) judgements about the magnitude of errors that could be found.

This formal approach closely parallels the usual audit process. It models the risk estimation problem facing the auditor who from an audit sample obtains two kinds of evidence. The first kind is about the error rate in the population and the second kind, from the sample items found to be in error, indicates the typical size of the errors. In the majority of well-controlled enterprises the auditor expects that the vast majority of account components will have zero error amounts. The auditor forms his prior view about the proportion of items in error based on his previous experience and from his review and testing of the internal control procedures. As we have seen the β family of distributions form a convenient set of template priors for making judgements about proportions.

For the second component of the formal model the auditor has to form a judgement about the average size of the error, μ, and of the spread or standard deviation, σ, of these errors about their average value. Judgements about the mean error size are linked to judgements about the variability of errors. Where there is expected to be a wide range of error amounts, then one must feel less confident in one's judgement about the size of the average error, than when the standard deviation is believed to be small.

The model for beliefs about error magnitudes is notationally quite complex, although conceptually quite intuitive. The model comes from the normal-γ-2 family of conjugate priors. To select a member of this family the auditor has to provide four parameters. These are derived from:

(i)   the best *a priori* estimate of the average error;
(ii)   how many observations this is worth as an equivalent prior sample;
(iii)   the best *a priori* estimate of the standard deviation of errors; and
(iv)   how many observations this is worth as an equivalent prior sample.

To implement the model using something like Novick's computer-assisted data-analysis (CADA) program,[9] the auditor could provide his four parameters by being conversationally interrogated until he is happy with the quantification of his prior judgements. An extract of such a computer assisted analysis is given in Appendix A6.1. As before, the technique for confirming the choice of conjugate prior would be to feed back 50% betting intervals, and other summary statistics.

For illustration, suppose an auditor's prior judgement was that if there were errors in a particular accounting population then they would have an average value of zero (i.e. overstatements would net out with understatements), and that this prior judgement was worth 16 observations. Furthermore, the standard deviation of these errors would be £12 000, and that this prior judgement was equivalent to six observations. Then these quantifications imply that the largest single error hidden in the population is about £30 000, and that there is a 50 : 50 chance that the average value of the errors would be greater than £2000. If the auditor was content with these implications then he would confirm his choice of parameters to model his prior judgement. Clearly the optimal manner for quantifying these prior judgements in an audit context and the design of user-friendly software to support this task is worthy of further experimentation and research.

The normal-γ-2 family of conjugate priors is formed by the product of a normal distribution which models beliefs about μ, the average size of the errors, and a γ distribution which models beliefs about h, the precision of the errors. Precision is the reciprocal of the variance ($h = \sigma^{-2}$) and the terms are used interchangeably. In notation, the two components of the model are represented as:

$$f_{Ng}(\mu,h) = f_N(\mu \mid m, hk) \times f_g(h \mid u, v) \qquad (6.1)$$

where $f_N(\cdot)$ is a normal distribution with parameters m and h and k and $f_g(\cdot)$ is a γ-distribution with parameters u and v. This scheme is set out diagrammatically in Figure 6.3.

When sample evidence is collected it is used to revise judgements in a straightforward way. A sample size n is taken which, on checking, is found to contain $(n-k)$ items that are error-free, and k items that are in error. The magnitude of each error is denoted by x_i. The sufficient statistics for updating the prior normal-γ-2 distributions are the sum of the errors, the sum of the squared errors, and the total number of errors. The beliefs after incorporating the sample evidence will also be normal-γ-2 with the new posterior parameters calculated in a straightforward manner.[10]

The observation of the k errors in a sample of N would also be used to revise the β prior about the proportion of errors of population. The posterior distribution, after incorporating the sample evidence, will then describe the defensible audit judgement about the size of the error in an accounting population.

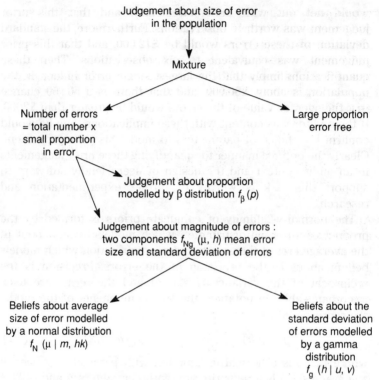

Figure 6.3. Felix and Grimlund's model of an accounting population.[1]

6.4 Simplification

This discussion is rather abstract. However, with some simplifications we can develop our intuition about Felix and Grimlund's model before looking at a practical application. If we assume that the proportion, p, of items in the accounting population under scrutiny in error is known, then we do not have the complication of a β distribution to weight judgements about p. For simplicity let us assume $p = 1$. If we further simplify the model by assuming that the standard deviation of the errors is known, then we further lose the γ distribution to model judgement weights about precision. The Bayesian treatment of the mean difference estimator has now been simplified to inferences about an unknown mean and known variance. To make our exposition even more concrete we apply the model to Bailey's inventory valuation problem.[11]

A client reports stock values totalling £400 000. Through the use of a generalized audit software package, an audit tape of the account value has been created and the following values established:

> Number of accounts, $N = 2000$
> Reported aggregate account value, $X = $ £400 000
> Average (mean per unit) reported account = £200
> Standard deviation of account values around value their mean £28

An auditor's prior judgement is that the total error will be neither an overstatement nor an understatement. There will be errors but the understatements will net-off with the overstatements. The mean difference between the book and audit value is expected to be zero ($m' = 0$). How confident is the auditor in this prior judgement? When pressed for a 50% betting interval he suggests plus or minus £10 000. That is the total error is just as likely to be more than £10 000 (either over or under) as it is to be less than £10 000 in absolute amount. The best point estimate and a 50% betting interval are all that are needed in order to select an appropriate member of the normal family of distributions to quantify these prior beliefs.

The normal distributions are a family of symmetrical bell-shaped curves, indexed by two parameters: the mean which gives the central location of the curve and the standard deviation, which gives the spread of the curve. As was stated earlier, the spread of the curve is sometimes measured by the precision, h, which is the reciprocal of the variance. The area under the curve corresponds to the probability or judgement weight. The normal distribution has so many applications that contemporary professional students cannot fail to have encountered tables which give the area under the curve for z standard deviations away from the mean. For example 25% of the area is included between the mean and 0.67 standard deviations from the mean. The auditor's prior judgement for Bailey's inventory valuation problem can be expressed graphically as shown in Figure 6.4.

The 50% betting interval of $\pm$£10 000 corresponds to $\pm 0.67\sigma'$.

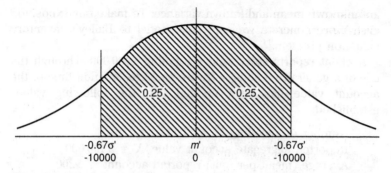

-0.67σ'   m'   -0.67σ'
-10000   0   -10000

Figure 6.4. Prior judgement for Bailey's inventory valuation problem.

Therefore $\sigma' = 10\,000/0.67 = £14\,925$. The auditor's prior judgement about the total error in the stock is thus modelled by a normal distribution with the parameters $m' = 0$ and $\sigma' = £14\,925$.

It is more convenient to talk in terms of the average size of the error per account, by dividing by the number of accounts ($N = 2000$). The prior on the mean difference is thus

$$f_N(\mu \mid m' = 0, \sigma' = 7.46)$$

or, equivalently, in terms of precision

$$f_N(\mu \mid m' = 0, h' = 0.018) \tag{6.2}$$

The very low value of h' indicates that the auditor's prior judgement is not very precise.

Now let us revise the prior in the light of audit evidence. An unrestricted sample of 30 accounts is now drawn and the result of checking is provided in Table 6.1 (columns 1–3). The sample mean difference is £5.9174 and the sum of the squared audit differences around their mean is £2604.3202. Audit evidence from the sample must be incorporated with the audit evidence that is quantified in the prior judgement.

The revision of judgement in the light of evidence is performed using the Bayes' result that the posterior is equal to the prior times the likelihood. The algebra is tedious to replicate, but readers who dislike results without derivation should consult Hey.[12] Here we rely on the standard results that the posterior beliefs are also modelled by a member of the normal family of distributions but with revised parameters as follows:

$$m'' = \frac{h'}{h' + h_m}m' + \frac{h_m}{h' + h_m}m \qquad (6.3)$$

$$h'' = h' + h_m \qquad (6.4)$$

The prior mean and precision m' and h' are tranformed into the up-dated parameters m'' and h'', using values which are calculated from the evidence. The sample mean, m, is 5.9174 and h_m is the sample precision of the mean. The sample precision of the mean is related to the standard error of the mean ($h_m = \sigma_m^{-2}$) where

$$\sigma_m^{-2} = \frac{S^2}{(k-1)k}$$

and S^2 is the sum of the squared differences around the mean and k is the sample size. Thus the sample precision is

$$h_m = \frac{(k-1)k}{S^2} = \frac{29 \times 30}{2604.3202} = 0.334$$

The posterior parameters accordingly are calculated thus:

$$m'' = \frac{0.018}{0.018 + 0.334} \times 0 + \frac{0.334}{0.018 + 0.334} 5.9174$$

$$= 5.6148$$

$$h'' = 0.352 \text{ (equivalently } \sigma''^2 = 2.84 \text{ and } \sigma'' = 1.6855)$$

These values now summarize the auditor's judgement about the average errors in the stock value. The effect of the evidence is for the auditor to change his mind about the average size of the error. The judgement about the total error in the inventory is obtained by multiplying the posterior belief by $N = 2000$; the audit judgement is thus modelled by

$$f_N \, (\mu \mid m'' = \text{\pounds}11\,229, \, \sigma'' = \text{\pounds}3371)$$

A 50% betting interval ($m'' \pm 0.67 \, \sigma''$) now ranges from a total

Table 6.1. Inventory valuation demonstration data.*

Sample item no., n_i	Account no.	Reported account value, x_i ($)	Audited account value, y_i ($)	$(y_i - \bar{y})^2$	Audit differences, $d_i = y_i - x_i$ ($)	$(d_i - \bar{d})^2$
1	2545	161.21	168.69	1317.8352	+7.48	2.4430
2	3988	193.68	174.53	927.9334	−9.15	227.0145
3	3825	246.80	255.70	2571.3013	+8.90	8.8983
4	2613	207.28	208.46	12.0270	+1.18	22.4392
5	3071	169.52	180.12	618.6164	+10.60	21.9305
6	2848	180.26	189.76	232.0138	+9.50	12.8379
7	3207	221.28	227.55	508.8634	+6.27	0.1246
8	2109	185.58	174.61	923.0659	−10.97	285.1708
9	2299	236.34	243.62	67.9965	+7.28	1.8578
10	3052	202.44	209.35	18.9922	+6.91	0.9860
11	2486	184.76	198.66	40.0942	+13.90	63.7283
12	2822	191.21	198.51	42.0163	+7.30	1.9127
13	3818	198.68	219.76	218.0938	+20.90	224.4903

		x	y	$\Sigma(y_i-y)^2$	d	$\Sigma(d_i-d)^2$
14	3674	192.65	208.46	12.0270	+15.81	97.8714
15	2304	210.83	214.12	83.3204	+3.29	6.9011
16	3206	208.59	219.41	207.8787	+10.82	24.0394
17	3659	205.98	215.83	117.4622	+9.85	15.4685
18	3544	148.35	172.39	1062.8904	+24.04	328.4431
19	3666	197.77	192.84	147.6711	-4.93	117.6574
20	3937	238.25	249.08	1943.7517	+10.83	24.1376
21	3187	244.85	231.89	723.5024	-12.96	356.3411
22	2622	192.28	191.72	176.1460	-0.56	41.9515
23	2530	179.93	172.80	1036.3249	-7.13	170.2242
24	2320	180.81	187.11	319.7659	+6.30	0.1467
25	2943	194.53	192.32	160.5796	-2.21	66.0481
26	3670	216.40	221.92	286.5572	+5.52	0.1576
27	3506	201.34	219.25	203.2906	+17.91	143.6320
28	2416	212.00	204.39	0.3624	-7.61	182.9797
29	2135	190.21	201.51	12.1243	+11.30	28.9767
30	3181	188.29	205.40	0.1665	+17.11	152.2832
Total Averages		5972.28 $x=\$199.076$	6149.76 $y=\$204.992$	13992.6708	177.51 $d=\$5.9174$	2604.3202

* From Bailey.[11]

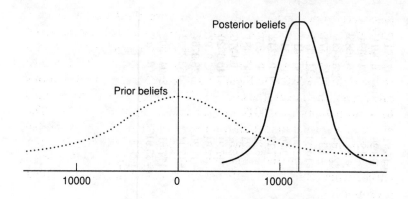

Figure 6.5. Posterior judgement for Bailey's inventory valuation problem.

error of £8971 to £13 487. These posterior beliefs are shown graphically in Figure 6.5.

The effect of taking evidence is to 'mass' the judgement weight. The width of the prior 50% betting interval was £20 000, whereas the width of the interval after incorporating the evidence is reduced to £6740. The auditor is more confident in his judgement. He believes that the stock value is understated. By how much is it understated? What is a true and fair estimate? As we saw in the last chapter the answer to this depends on the loss function the auditor faces. If he believes that his losses (costs) for understating the size of the error are 50 times more than for overstatement, then he needs a 50/51 fractile of his posterior distribution. From tables this corresponds to 2.06 standard deviations away from the mean, giving an error of (11 229 + 2.06 × 3371) = £18 173. Thus to this auditor the understatement of stock is £18 173. Should he require management to change its asserted value of £400 000? Again, as we have discussed, this depends on the materiality limits. Suppose he had decided that 5% was material, then his judgement would correspond to case B of Chapter 4, i.e. do not adjust.

The model enables the auditor to quantify his risk of making a so-called type II error or his β risk, i.e. accepting an assertion that no material deviation exists, when the contrary is the case. This type of error, it will be recalled, is not usually immediately

discovered once made. If discovered after the financial reports
have been issued the cost to the auditor can be substantial since
he will have certified something incorrectly. In this example, with
5% materiality limits on £400 000 the β risk is given by the area
to the right of £20 000 in Figure 6.6. This is 2.6 standard deviations
away from the mean ((20 000 − 11 229)/3371) which corresponds
to a probability of 0.0047 or just under 1 chance in 200. The
effort of a formal model allows risk judgements to be quantified
and compared. Although we are dealing with magnitudes, our
model operates in the same intuitive way which we discussed
earlier when considering attribute testing and judgements about
a proportion.

The intuition of Felix and Grimlund's model can be explored
further by representing the posterior judgement as follows:

$$f_N\left(m'' = wm' + (1 - w)\,m, h'' = h' + h_m\right) \qquad (6.5)$$

The revised mean m'' is a weighted average of the prior mean
m' and the sample mean m. The weight w is the ratio of the
prior precision to the posterior precision ($w = h'/h''$). The
posterior precision is in turn the sum of the prior and sample
precisions where the sample precision

$$h_m = \sigma_m^{-2} = \frac{(k - 1)k}{S^2} = \frac{k}{\theta^2} \qquad (6.6)$$

where

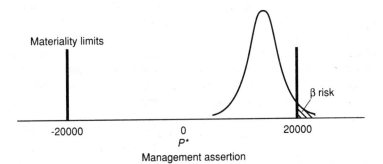

Figure 6.6. The β risk for inventory valuation.

$$\theta^2 = \frac{S^2}{k-1} = \frac{1}{k-1}\Sigma\,(x_i - m)^2 \qquad (6.7)$$

and θ is the standard deviation of errors, which is assumed known. The posterior precision can also be written

$$h'' = h' + \frac{k}{\theta^2} \qquad (6.8)$$

Several properties of this model follow from equations (6.5) and (6.8).

(i) As the sample of errors (i.e. k) increases so does the posterior precision. This is a useful property since increasing precision implies decreasing standard deviation and decreasing spread of the normal distribution. Reducing the spread or 'massing' the distribution means that one is less vague in one's judgement. So an increase in the amount of evidence about the errors leads to a reduction in uncertainty. This is a sensible property of the model. In the limit as the number of errors found becomes very large indeed, so does the precision with which they are estimated, conversely the standard deviation gets very small. When there is no uncertainty remaining in judgement about the size of errors, the standard deviation is zero.

(ii) A zero precision (an infinite standard deviation) corresponds to a totally vague prior. When $h' = 0$, it follows that $w = 0$ so no weight at all is given to prior beliefs, and judgement depends entirely on sample evidence (i.e. $m'' = m$ and $h'' = h_m$). Ignoring prior beliefs and making judgements entirely on sample evidence is the approach of classic statistics, which has hitherto been the dominant paradigm in statistical education and, in consequence, in statistical auditing.

(iii) When an auditor has prior beliefs with some precision h', it may be deemed equivalent to having started originally with a totally vague prior and to have already taken an audit sample. That is, from equation (6.8)

$$h' = 0 + \frac{k_0}{\theta^2}$$

With θ^2 known, an auditor expressing his 'nose' in terms of a prior precision of h' is equivalent to considering that his prior judgement is worth k_0 observations ($k_0 = h'\theta^2$). [In this model the equivalent prior sample size is an important parameter because errors are rare, and it is expensive to increase the number of errors discovered because this requires significantly increasing the actual sample size. In the full model there is a distinction between the total number of items which an auditor tests, n, and the number of errors, k, which are discovered. Our assumption that $p = 1$ removes this complication]. The key to the potential cost savings of this model lies in giving due weight to all the prior work and to the related tests that have been performed. The method explicitly values related tests in terms of an equivalent prior sample.

(iv) Posterior beliefs about the size of the error depend on both prior judgements and sample evidence, i.e. from equation (6.5)

$$m'' = wm' + (1 - w)\, m$$

The model consistently balances the two. As the posterior precision h'' increases, so the weight w given to prior beliefs reduces. In the limit as the posterior precision gets very large, all the weight about the size of the error comes from the actual samples.

(v) The model also explains how one must set a sample size, in order to control for risk. The important risk to control is of type II errors, or β risk. The risk of a type II error is calculated in the model as the judgement weight outside the materiality range. The area under the judgement curve falling outside the materiality interval can be reduced by reducing the spread of the curve. Reducing the spread or standard deviation implies increasing the precision. As observed earlier, as the sample size increases so does the precision. We can connect these links to obtain a formula for relating the target sample size to the target risk. Planning to make β risk very small involves making the materiality range into a very high betting interval. For example, a 5% risk of error implies believing that there is a 95% chance that the error is within the materiality limits. From tables of the normal distribution, we know that 95% of the area lies within ± 1.96 standard deviations from the mean. For the materiality range to correspond to a 95% betting interval it needs to be equivalent to 2×1.96 standard deviations. In general,

$$m_i = 2\,Z_\beta \sigma'' \tag{6.9}$$

where m_i is the materiality range, σ'' is the posterior standard deviation, and Z_β is the number of standard deviations needed to give $(1 - \beta)$ of the judgement weight inside the range, and β outside.

Combining equation (6.9) with earlier results, $\sigma''^{-2} = h''$, $h'' = h' + \dfrac{k}{\theta^2}$ and $h' = \dfrac{k_0}{\theta^2}$ (equation 6.8) gives

$$k_0 + k = \frac{Z_\beta{}^2}{(m_i/2)^2}\,\theta^2 \tag{6.10}$$

This formula relates the sample size k to the target or acceptable risk level indexed by Z_β, the width of the materiality interval m_i, where θ is the standard deviation of errors and k_0 is the equivalent prior sample size.

For illustration, if $\theta = £30\,000$, $m_i = £20\,000$ and $\beta = 5\%$ (i.e. $Z_\beta = 1.96$), then $k_0 + k = 35$. If prior beliefs are equivalent to (k_0) 10 observations, then the sample size (k) should be 25. The more weight that is placed on prior beliefs the smaller should be the actual sample tested. If the materiality interval had been £37 000 wide, then a sample size of zero would have been acceptable. The audit opinion in this case would have been based entirely on the prior beliefs. The required sample size is quite sensitive to the choice of materiality interval. If the materiality interval is halved, the sample size $(k + k_0)$ should quadruple because they are related by an inverse square law.

The sample size is, however, most sensitive to the target risk level, because of the way that $Z_\beta{}^2$ varies with the risk β (see Table 6.2). A 90% betting interval with a 10% β risk has $Z_\beta{}^2 = 2.6896$. If an auditor wanted to achieve a 99% betting interval on the same materiality range then the $Z_\beta{}^2$ would increase to 6.6049, implying a (6.6049/2.6896) sample size 2.5 times larger. A 99.8% betting interval would thus need a 3.5 times larger sample size. How many of us know the difference between 99% and 99.8% confidence, and how many would know the increased sample sizes that would be needed to increase confidence by 0.8 of a basis point?

Understanding the relationship between how much evidence to collect, giving proper weight to prior judgement, and balancing

Table 6.2. The relationship between β and Z_β^2.*

β risk (%)	Betting interval (%)	Z_β	Z_β^2
50	50	0.67	0.4489
40	60	0.84	0.7056
20	80	1.28	1.6384
10	90	1.64	2.6896
5	95	1.96	3.8416
2	98	2.32	5.3824
1	99	2.57	6.6049
0.2	99.8	3.08	9.4864
0.006	99.994	4.00	16.0000

* Taken from tables of the normal distribution.

decisions about materiality with the risk of error is one of the important practical problems an auditor faces. Equation (6.10) is an important result for giving insight into this problem. Misallocation of audit evidence resources (either under- or over-auditing) comes from insufficiently adjusting planning guidelines as circumstances vary. The formal model we have described allows the factors that affect this judgement to be considered explicitly.

6.5 Practical illustration

We are now in a position to describe the operation of Felix and Grimlund's full model.[1] In the simplified example given in the previous section, we assumed that the variance of the process generating the errors was known. The results discussed were for an error process with an unknown mean, but known variance. In considering the situation in which both parameters are unknown, the auditors' prior judgement about the mean size of the error is linked to judgements about the variance of the errors. For illustration, in forming a view about an unreliable system for pricing stock, if the items are priced using a wide range of inaccurate values (i.e. large error variance) then the confidence one could have in the mean error size would be lower than if the error variance were smaller. The prior on the mean difference would have a very low precision, and the precision would depend on the error variance. In general, judgement about the mean error size depends on judgements about the variance of the error process. Thus, continuing the illustration of an auditor forming a judgement about an unreliable stock pricing system, the presence of an exception reporting internal control which identified over-stocked product lines by comparing budgeted sales values against stock holdings might have the effect of reducing the range of errors, because any large exceptions might be investigated. Reducing the range of errors, in turn reduces their variance, and would increase the auditor's confidence in his judgement about the mean error and hence the total size of error in the inventory. (Improving the reliability of an accounting system can mean reducing the variance of uncorrected errors.)

In the full model, judgement involves two distributions: a β

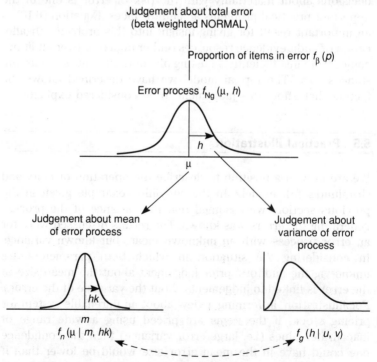

Figure 6.7. Conjugate priors in Felix and Grimlund's model.

distribution for modelling beliefs about the error rate or proportion of items in error; and a normal-γ -2 distribution for modelling beliefs about the error process. The process by which errors are generated in the population is assumed to be well described by a normal distribution. Audit judgement involves quantifying belief about both the mean of this normal distribution, and also its variance. The normal-γ -2 distribution provide a family of conjugate priors for beliefs about the mean and variance of a normal distribution. The scheme is set out in Figure 6.7: judgement about the mean error size is linked to judgement about the variance of the error process.

Felix and Grimlund illustrate their model with the evaluation of a population of 5000 items. The first audit test comprised 100 items in which three errors were discovered with differences between the book amount and the audited amount of $-£13.51$, £79.17 and £114.11. A second sample of 100 was then tested and a further two errors were discovered amounting to £4.20 and $-£4.72$.

The auditor's judgement of the total error in the accounting population, and how this evidence is evaluated depends on prior judgement. Three cases are discussed in the original paper: the first is where an auditor has strong prior beliefs that the error rate is low, the second illustration is of a moderately informative prior with a higher error rate, and the third case evaluates the audit samples with a non-informative or vague prior. Here we describe only their first case. Prior audit judgement about the error rate is described by a β distribution with the parameters $a = 2$ and $b = 298$ (NB as discussed in Appendix 6.2 a slightly different notation convention is used in the original paper). This has a mean error rate (see Chapter 5) of 2/300 and a modal error rate of 1/298 or about 1 error in every 300 items. Prior judgement about the average error size for the items in error is 20, and this is considered to be worth eight observations. The prior modal standard deviation of the error generating process is 40, the 75% percentile of this standard deviation is 50. This gives an equivalent prior sample on the standard deviation $v' = 6$. The parameters for the prior γ distribution are $u' = 1371.7$ and $v' = 6$.

Using the results discussed earlier, these prior beliefs are revised in the light of the evidence. The first sample revises the β density function to provide an intermediate posterior with the

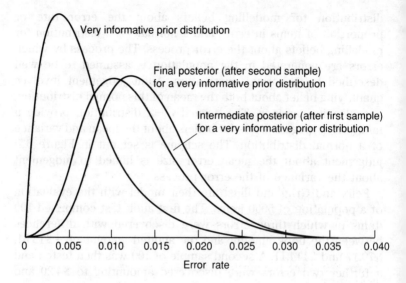

Figure 6.8.   The β density functions with a very informative prior error rate distribution.

parameters $a = 2 + 3 = 5$ and $b = 298 + 100 - 3 = 395$. After the second sample the final posterior is obtained with new parameters $(a = 5 + 2 = 7$ and $b = 395 + 100 - 2 = 493)$. This sequential revision of judgement about the error rate is shown in Figure 6.8.

The revision of judgement about the error process after the first sample gives the mean error size with the parameters $m = 30.90$ and $k = 11.0$, and the revision of the γ distribution with the new values $u'' = 2267.40$ and $v'' = 9.0$. The second sample leads to final posterior parameters on the mean error size of $m = 26.10$ and $k = 13$ and a γ distribution with $u'' = 2008.10$ and $v'' = 11.0$. The changing judgement weight associated with the total error amount is shown graphically in Figure 6.9.

The judgement about the size of the total error (see Appendix 6.2) in this model is described by a β weighted set of normal distributions:

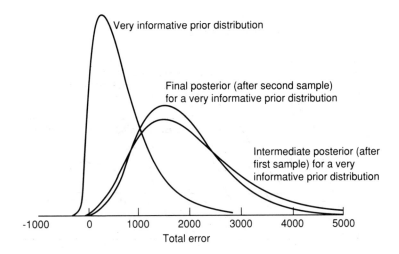

Figure 6.9. The β normal density functions with a very informative prior distribution.

$$f(\pi_r) = \int_0^1 f_\beta (p \mid a, b) f_N(rE(\pi), \frac{1}{r \operatorname{var}(\pi)}) \, dp$$

where $a = 7$ and $b = 497$, $r = p \times 5000$ is the expected number of errors in 5000 items where p is the error rate, $E(\pi)$ is the expected error size ($= m'' = 26.10$) and var (π) is the variance of the error process

$$\operatorname{var}(\pi) = \frac{v''}{(v''-2)} \frac{(1+k)}{k} u''$$

where for $v'' = 11$, $u'' = 2008.10$ and $k = 13.0$, var $(\pi) = 2643.14$.

This is an intriguing result in which the error size is given by a mixture of normal distributions, each with a different mean and variance which increases with the error rate p. The importance of each normal distribution in the mixture depends on the probability weight attached to its associated error rate p which, in turn, is given by a β distribution. The results are shown graphically in Figure 6.10.

The mixture property of Felix and Grimlund's model can be

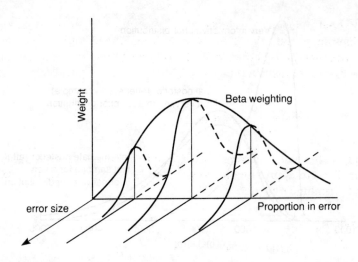

Figure 6.10. A set of β weighted normal distributions.

more clearly illustrated in this example by approximating the
weight given by a continuous β distribution to the equivalent
weight as massing at only three points (the first sextile, the third
sextile and the fifth sextile). Using the normal approximation to
the β distribution,

$$z = 2[x(b- 1/3)]^{\frac{1}{2}} - 2[(1 - x)(a- 1/3)]^{\frac{1}{2}}$$

where z is the appropriate sextile of the normal distribution
(-0.43, 0, 0.43), the corresponding sextiles of the β distribution
($a = 7$ and $b = 493$) and x can be found to be (0.01124, 0.01335,
0.01565).

Rather than weighting values of p in the continuous range (0,

Table 6.3. The discrete approximation of the β distribution.

	Range	Weight
Old	$0 \leq p \leq 1$	$kp^{a-1} (1-p)^{b-1}$ $a=7$, $b=493$
New	$p = 0.01124$	1/3
	$p = 0.01335$	1/3
	$p = 0.01565$	1/3

1), equal judgement weights of 1/3 are attached to these three values of p, thus the β function is transformed into a discrete approximation as shown in Table 6.3. This transformation affects the β normal distribution:

$$f(\pi_T) = \int_0^1 f_\beta(p \mid a,b) f_N\left(rE(\pi), \frac{1}{r\,\text{var}\,(\pi)}\right) dp$$

and, instead of requiring us to evaluate a continuous integral, our discrete approximation reveals the mixing property of Felix and Grimlund's model:

$$f(\pi_T) =$$
$$\frac{1}{3} \times f_N\left(0.01124 \times 5000 \times E(\pi),\ \frac{1}{0.01124 \times 5000 \times \text{var}\,(\pi)}\right)$$
$$+\ \frac{1}{3} \times f_N\left(0.01335 \times 5000 \times E(\pi),\ \frac{1}{0.01335 \times 5000 \times \text{var}\,(\pi)}\right)$$
$$+\ \frac{1}{3} \times f_N\left(0.011565 \times 5000 \times E(\pi),\ \frac{1}{0.01565 \times 5000 \times \text{var}\,(\pi)}\right)$$

$$f(\pi_T) =$$
$$\tfrac{1}{3} f_N\,(1466.82,\ 1/148544) + \tfrac{1}{3} f_N\,(1742.17,\ 1/176429) + \tfrac{1}{3} f_N\,(2042.32,\ 1/206825)$$

In this case judgement about the total error (π_T) is seen to be a mixture of three normal distributions with increasing means (1466.82, 1742.17 and 2042.32) and increasing standard deviations (385, 420 and 454). Figure 6.9, which Felix and Grimlund presented as encapsulating the combination of judgement and evidence about the size of the total error, can be compared to this representation (see Figure 6.11).

With judgement quantified in this way the auditor is on surer ground to decide what a 'true and fair' error amount is, or to calculate the β risk for some level of materiality. Unfortunately, evaluating the integrals involved is not as straightforward as in the simplified model discussed in Chapter 5 and the computations must be performed using a computer. The technical details of such computations take us beyond the central theme of this book, which is to review the major Bayesian contributions in

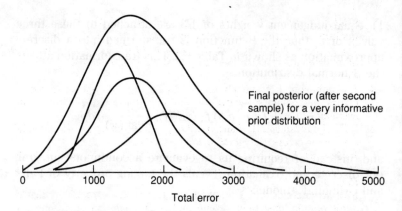

Figure 6.11. Final posterior as a mixture of normal distributions of increasing means and standard deviations.

auditing. The complexities of computation provide an interesting field of study in their own right. However, we can skate over this detail, as Felix and Grimlund themselves observe:

> Our analysis has been built up with extensive sets of notation, embodying numerous probability distributions and analytical results. We assume that the auditor has a readily accessible computer capability. In today's technological environments, these observations complement each other. Once a computing procedure is established, the operational aspects of utilizing the beta-normal procedure appear very straightforward for the well trained auditor. The few observed error amounts are the only tedious numbers that must be entered ... Much research must be done before Bayesian procedures can be effectively integrated into the auditing process. Our goal in this paper has been to push back one of the analytical frontiers constraining such procedures. As we have just emphasised, computational difficulties need not arise as we proceed to expand the power of our analytical tools.

Notes and references

1   W.L. Felix and R.A. Grimlund (1977) A sampling model for audit tests of composite accounts, *Journal of Accounting Research*, **Spring**, 23–41.
2   J. Neter and J.K. Loebbecke (1975) *Behaviour of Major Statistical Estimators in Sampling Accounting Populations—An Empirical*

Study, Auditing Research Monograph No. 2, (AICPA, American Institute of Certified Public Accountants.

3   J.G. Ramage, A.M. Krieger and L.L. Spero (1979) An empirical study of error characteristics in audit populations, *Journal of Accounting Research*, (Suppl.) 72–113.

4   J.R. Johnson, R.A. Leitch and J. Neter (1981) Characteristics of errors in accounts receivable and inventory audits, *Accounting Review*, 270–293.

5   R.E. Hylas and R.H. Ashton (1982) Audit detection of financial statement errors, *Accounting Review*, **Oct.**, 751–765.

6   J. Ham, D. Losell and W. Smieliauskas (1985) An empirical study of error characteristics in accounting populations, *Accounting Review*, **Jul.**, 387–406.

7   R.W. Kreutzfeldt and W.A. Wallace (1986) Error characteristics in audit populations: their profile and relationship to environmental factors, *Auditing: A Journal of Practice and Theory*, **Autumn**, 20–43.

8   R.S. Kaplan (1973) Statistical sampling in auditing with auxiliary information estimators, *Journal of Accounting Research*, **Autumn**, 238–258.

9   M.R. Novick and P.H. Jackson (1971) CADA program: see Figure 4.9 and Appendix 6.1.

10 If a sample of size n yields k errors where x_i (for $i = 1$ to k) are the observed error amounts, then the auditor's posterior β distribution for the error rate of the population has the parameters $a + k$ and $b + n - k$. The statistics for up-dating the normal-γ-2 distributions are

$$m = \frac{1}{k}\Sigma\, x_i, u = \frac{1}{k-1}\Sigma\,(x_i - m)^2$$

($u = 0$ if $k = 1$) and $v = k - 1$

The revised parameters will be

$$\text{m}'' = \frac{k'm' + km}{k' + k}$$

$$v'' = v' + v + 1 \text{ for } k' > 0$$

$$v' + v \text{ for } k' = 0$$

$$k'' = k' + k$$

$$u'' = \frac{[v'u' + k'm'^2] + [uv + km^2] - k''m''^2}{v}$$

where the double prime denotes the posterior parameters, the single prime the prior parameters, and the unprimed the sample statistics. See: H. Raiffa and R. Schlaifer (1961) *Applied Statistical Decision Theory*, pp. 300–301. Cambridge, MA: MIT Press.

11   A.D. Bailey (1981) *Statistical Auditing: Review, Concepts and Problems*, p. 124. New York: Harcourt Brace Jovanovich.
12   J.D. Hey (1983) Data in Doubt: An Introduction to Bayesian Statistical Inference for Economists, Chap. 6. Oxford: Blackwell.
13   M.R. Novick and P.H. Jackson (1974) *Statistical Methods for Educational and Psychological Research*, pp. 217–222. New York: McGraw-Hill.
14   See note 10.
15   J.D. Hey (1983) pp. 160–164. (see note 12).
16   Raiffa and Schlaiffer, p. 235 (see note 10).

APPENDIX 6.1
Computer assisted data analysis

The following extract is taken from Novick and Jackson.[13]

If you wish an explanation type 1, otherwise, type 0
?
1
This packet of programs provides a grounding in the fundamentals of Bayesian methods of statistical inference. These routines are designed to guide the researcher who has only a minimal acquaintance with Bayesian methods, step-by-step through a complete Bayesian analysis, a list of the routine follows:

1.   prior β-binomial model
2.   posterior β-binomial model
3.   Prior two-parameter normal-marginal distribution for standard deviation
4.   Prior two-parameter normal-conditional distribution for mean
5.   Posterior two-parameter normal
6.   Prior m-group proportions
7.   Posterior m-group proportions
8.   Evaluate student distribution
9.   Evaluate β-distribution
10. Evaluate inverse χ-distribution
11. Evaluate normal distribution

If you want to run one of the above routines, type its number. Otherwise, type a zero.

?
3

This program will assist you in specifying a prior distribution on the standard deviation.

Considering your prior information, what do you feel is the most probable value of the standard deviation?
?
4.9

Now viewing your information about the standard deviation as if it were the result of an experiment of a certain sample size (n), how large an n value do you feel your prior information to be worth? This n value is the amount of weight that will be given to your prior knowledge and should be greater than 6.
?
7

[Inexperienced investigators are typically very conservative in their specification of n. When they see the length of the 50% credibility interval implied by their value, they typically increase this value.]

The value of n and your estimate of the standard deviation imply that you would be willing to give even odds that the true standard deviation will lie in the 50% hdr credibility interval from 4.029 to 6.117. This is the shortest possible 50% credibility interval for this value of n.
If you think you may be able to improve this interval by selecting a new value of n, please type that value, otherwise, type zero.
?
20

The new 50% credibility interval, based on an n of 20.00 extends from 4.390 to 5.494. The old 50% credibility based on an n of 7.00 extends from 4.029 to 6.117. If you think you can improve this interval by selecting a new value of n, please type that value, otherwise, type 0.
?
25

The new 50% credibility interval, based on an n of 25.00 extends from 4.452 to 5.428.
The old 50% credibility based on an n of 20.00 extends from 4.390 to 5.494.
If you think you can improve this interval by selecting a new value of n, please type that value, otherwise, type 0.
?
0

On the basis of the information so far given, the prior marginal distribution of the standard deviation is an inverse χ with 24.00 degrees of freedom and a scale parameter of 24.500. This distribution has a mode of 4.900 a median of 5.072 and a mean of 5.165. A 50% credibility interval extends from 4.452 to 5.428.

> [The value of n typically settled on is one that implies a somewhat longer interval than the investigator would have initially specified. By requiring the investigator to balance two judgements against each other, we hope to arrive at a coherent and realistic assessment.]

If you think that you may be able to obtain a better prior distribution by respecifying your modal estimate of the standard deviation, please type your new estimate, otherwise, type 0.
?
4.7

> [This is one of several points at which the investigator can change his mind about some aspect of his prior beliefs. This is a particularly useful point. Most investigators are unappreciative of the asymmetry of the inverse χ density, and thus are surprised by the length above the model required to obtain a 50% hdr interval. A typical desire, at this point, is to lower the modal estimate slightly.]

Now viewing your information about the standard deviation as if it were the result of an experiment of a certain sample size (n), how large an n value do you feel your prior information to be worth? This n value is the amount of weight that will be given to your prior knowledge and should be greater than 6.
?
20

The value of n and your estimate of the standard deviation imply that you would be willing to give even odds that the true standard deviation will lie in the 50% hdr credibility interval from 4.211 to 5.269. This is the shortest possible 50% credibility interval for this value of n.

Consider the above interval. It may or may not be satisfactory to you. You may increase the interval by selecting a small n, or decrease the interval by selecting a larger n.
If you think you may be able to improve this interval by selecting a new value of n, please type that value, otherwise type zero.
?
0

On the basis of the information so far given, the prior marginal distribution of the standard deviation is an inverse χ with 19.00 degrees of freedom and a scale parameter of 21.019. This distribution has a mode of 4.700 a median of 4.909 and a mean of 5.025. A 50% credibility interval extends from 4.211 to 5.269.

If you think you may be able to obtain a better prior distribution by respecifying your modal estimate of the standard deviation, please type your new estimate, otherwise, type zero.
?
0

Do you wish to specify a prior on the mean at this time? If so type 1, otherwise type zero.
?
1

This program will, given your modal estimate of the standard deviation and the number of observations it is worth, assist you in fitting your prior conditional distribution on the mean to a normal distribution.

What is your modal estimate of the standard deviation?
?
4.7

How many observations is your estimate worth?
?
20

Now considering your prior information about the mean and assuming your modal estimate of the standard deviation is the actual true value, what is your best estimate of the true value of the unknown mean?
?
21

Suppose I estimated a certain mean to be 100 and was willing to give even odds that the true mean would be between 95 and 105, then my central 50% credibility interval would be 10 units long.

How long would a central interval around your estimate of the mean for the present problem need to be for you to be willing to give even odds that the true mean will lie in this interval?
?
2

Considering your prior knowledge as if it were the result of an experiment of a certain sample of size m, how many observations do you feel your prior knowledge about the mean to be worth?
?
5

The value of m you selected implies a 50% credibility interval extending from 19.582 to 22.418 ($m = 5.00$). The original interval specified, which implies $m = 10.00$ extends from 20.000 to 22.000.

> [Having treated the investigator gently in the first part of the program, we now attempt to show him that coherence in prior specifications is difficult to attain. The present investigator displays a rather high degree of coherence at this point compared with others who have used this program.]

Please compare these two intervals. If your original interval is longer than the interval resulting from your selection of m, you may wish to select a smaller value of m. If your interval is small, you may wish to select a larger value of m. However, such changes will affect the weight you will be giving to your prior information.

If you are satisfied with the interval extending from 19.582 to 22.418 ($m = 5.00$), please type 0. Otherwise, select a new value for m. Presumably you will want to select some value between $m = 5.00$ and $m = 10.00$ although you are free to select any positive value you wish.

?

8

The new interval around your estimated mean with $m = 8.00$ extends from 19.879 to 22.121. Your original interval around the mean with $m = 10.00$ extends from 20.000 to 22.000.

If you think you can improve your present interval by selecting a new value for m, please type that value, otherwise type 0.

?

10

The new interval around your estimated mean with $m = 10.00$ extends from 19.998 to 22.002. Your original interval around the mean with $m = 10.00$ extends from 20.000 to 22.000.

If you think you can improve your present interval by selecting a new value for m, please type that value. Otherwise type 0.

?

0

Your prior conditional distribution or the mean (given that the true standard deviation of 4.700 is normal, with a mean of 21.000 a variance of 2.209 and a standard deviation of 1.486. The 50% credibility interval around the mean extends from 19.998 to 22.002.

Your prior marginal distribution on the mean is a students distribution on 19.00 degrees of freedom, with mean, mode and median of 21.000 and standard deviation 1.612 the 50% credibility interval about the mean extends from 19.951 to 22.049.

APPENDIX 6.2
Key results for Felix and Grimlund model

The notation in the original paper is both complex and, unfortunately, has some minor, inevitable typographical errors. The conventions employed are that unprimed letters represent sufficient statistics derived from sample evidence, single-primed letters denote prior parameters for the conjugate prior distributions, and double-primed letters represent posterior parameters.

The letters used are:

> sample size n
> number of errors in sample k
> size of observed error amounts x_i
>
> sample mean size of error $m = \dfrac{1}{k} \Sigma x_i$
>
> sample error variance $\quad u = \dfrac{1}{k-1} \Sigma (x_i - m)^2$
>
> $\qquad\qquad\qquad (u = 0 \text{ if } k = 1)$
>
> $\qquad\qquad\qquad v = k - 1$

The error rate of the population is p. The auditor's prior β distribution for the error rate of the population that Felix and Grimlund use has parameters $a = k'$ and $b = n' - k'$. This formulation differs from the parameterization we have used to describe the β distribution, although its equivalence is obvious:

$$f_\beta(p \mid k', n') \;\propto\; p^{k'-1}(1-p)^{n'-k'-1}$$

The mean of the error process is μ, the precision of the error process is $h = 1/\sigma^2$ where σ^2 is the variance of the error process.

Beliefs about the error process are modelled by a joint distribution

$$f_{Ng}(\mu, h \mid m', u', k'_n, v')$$

where the four parameters m', u', k'_n and v' relate to a normal conditional distribution on the mean μ of the process

$$f_N(\mu \mid m', \; hk'_n)$$

and a γ marginal distribution on the precision h of the process

$$f_g(h \mid u', v')$$

and

$$f_{Ng}(\mu, h \mid m', u', k_n', v') = f_N(\mu \mid m', hk'_n) f_g(h \mid u', v')$$

where

$$f_N(\mu \mid m', hk_n') \propto (hk'_n)^{\frac{1}{2}} \exp\left[-\tfrac{1}{2}(m' - \mu)^2 hk'_n\right]$$

and

$$f_g(h \mid u', v') \propto h^{v'-1} \exp(-u'h)$$

Incorporating the sample evidence into the prior beliefs leads to posterior beliefs whose parameters are given as follows:

revision of the β distribution

$$k'' = k' + k$$
$$n'' = n' + n$$

revision of the normal distribution

$$k''_n = k'_n + k$$

$$m'' = \frac{k'_n m' + km}{k''_n}$$

revision of the γ distribution

$$v'' = v' + k \text{ for } k'_n > 0$$

$$v'' = v' + k - 1 \text{ for } k'_n = 0$$

$$u'' = \frac{[v'u' + k'_n m'^2] + [uv + km^2] - k''_n m''^2}{v''}$$

The derivation of these results is given in Raiffa and Schlaiffer[14] and Hey.[15]

The size of an error (π) is assumed to arise from a error-generating process which is normal $f_N(\pi \mid \mu, h)$, thus the marginal density for π is

$$f(\pi) = \int_0^\infty \int_{-\infty}^\infty f_N(\pi \mid \mu, h) f_N(\mu \mid m'', k_n''h) f_g(h \mid u'', v'') \, d\mu \, dh$$

This has a generalized Student distribution with mean $E(\mu) = m''$ and variance

$$\text{var}\,(\pi) = \frac{v''}{(v''-2)}\frac{(1+k''_n)}{k''_n}\,u''$$

for $v'' > 2$ (for a derivation see Raiffa and Schlaiffer).[16]

The sum of independent drawings from a Student distribution is approximately normal. Thus if there are r errors then the total error in the population, π_T, will be approximately normal (i.e. $\pi_T = \pi_1 + \pi_2 + \pi_3 + \ldots \pi_r$, where each π_i has a Student distribution)

$$f(\pi_T \mid r) = f_N\left(rE\,(\pi),\frac{1}{r\,\text{var}\,(\pi)}\right)$$

This gives the conditional distribution of π_T given the number of errors r. With a β distribution describing judgement about the proportion of errors p, if the total number of items in the population is X, then $r = pX$ (approximating a discrete r by a continuous variable p). It follows that the unconditional distribution of π_T is given by:

$$f(\pi_T) = \int_0^1 f_\beta\,(p \mid k'',n'')f_N\left(rE(\pi),\frac{1}{r\,\text{var}\,(\pi)}\right)\mathrm{d}p$$

This is the key result of the Felix and Grimlund model. Uncertainty about the total error in the population is modelled by a set of normal distributions each weighted by a β distribution. The mean for each normal distribution and its variance increases with the error proportion. Felix and Grimlund observed that the expression cannot be simply evaluated, instead they developed an approximation based on matching the moments of $f(\pi_T)$ with the moments of a known γ distribution.

Chapter 7

Substantive Testing: Error Bounds

7.1 Introduction

In Chapter 6 we discussed a model for auditors' beliefs about the size of errors in an accounting population. This enabled us to consider how judgement about rare errors can be modelled as judgements about mixtures of populations—a small tainted one mixed with a larger error-free one. In the Felix and Grimlund[1] model, the auditor achieved a posterior distribution which combined his prior judgement with his sample evidence, in order to describe fully his judgement about the size of the error. Judgements were needed about the average size of the errors and of the proportion of errors in the population. In this chapter we draw the connections between this approach and monetary unit sampling bounds. In monetary sampling the auditor does not seek to describe his judgement fully, but instead aims to make more limited statements about the maximum size of the error. If π_T is the total error in the accounting population, and beliefs about π_T are modelled by a weight function $f(\pi_T)$ then, as shown in Chapter 6, these beliefs can be split into constituent parts:

$$f(\pi_T) = N \times f_\beta(p) \times f_{Ng}(\mu, h)$$

where N is the number of items in the accounting population, $f_\beta(p)$ are the beliefs about the proportion p of the items in error, and $f_{Ng}(\mu, h)$ are the beliefs about the average size of the individual errors that occur.

The judgement weight that the total error is larger than some amount π_T^* is given as the area under the judgement curve, which is denoted by

$$\int_{-\infty}^{\pi_T^*} f(\pi_T) d\pi_T = (1-\alpha)$$

which could be read as 'the probability that the total error is greater than amount π_T^* is α'; or, conversely, 'I am $(1-\alpha)100\%$ certain that the total error is no larger than π_T^*'; or 'the amount π_T^* is the $(1-\alpha)100$th percentile of the posterior distribution'. In monetary unit sampling the approach is not to model posterior judgement directly but to estimate a bound B on the $(1-\alpha)100$th percentile.

In order to err on the safe side, the amount B is chosen as an over-estimate so that the $(1-\alpha)100$th percentile is less than B. Audit opinions are then expressed as: 'I am at least $(1-\alpha)100\%$ certain that the total error is no larger than B'. This is done not by judging the average size of errors and their frequency, but by estimating the largest size of error and the greatest frequency by which they could occur. In choosing the worst cases in this way, the bound B can be excessively cautious and prudent, which can in turn lead to over-auditing. Our exposition draws on Fienberg *et al.*[2] We describe first a simple, but very conservative error bound. Subsequently, we discuss how stratification can tighten this bound. This leads into an exposition of stratification by monetary units. We look at sample size determination and comment on the American Institute of Certified Public Accountants (AICPA) audit risk model, before turning to the problem of combining attributes and variable sampling. Of the solutions to this problem, we expound the quasi-Bayesian bound method proposed by McCray.[3]

7.2 Simple bound

When an auditor examines a set of accounts he typically knows the book values $Y_1, Y_2, \ldots Y_n$ in the population. The total book value is denoted by Y. If there were a 100% audit, then he would obtain a set of audit values $X_1, X_2, \ldots X_n$. If the total audit value is X, then the total error would be

$$\pi_T = Y - X$$

Typically the auditor only audits a sample of accounts, in order to form a judgement $f(\pi_T)$ about the weight he would attach to various errors.

If we assume that the auditor is only concerned about overstatement errors, and we further assume that the maximum overstatement for any individual account item $\pi_i = Y_i - X_i$ is the amount of the book balance, i.e. $\pi_i = Y_i$ when $X_i = 0$. Then the largest account book balance in the population Y_L will be an upper bound on the average size of individual errors, since no overstatement error in the population can exceed Y_L. Turning to the second component, the judgement about the proportion that are in error, the $(1-\alpha)100$th percentile of $f_\beta(p)$ can be used.

$$\int_0^{p*} f_\beta(p)\mathrm{d}p = 1-\alpha$$

If p^* is the required percentile, then the upper bound on the total error is:

$$B = N Y_L p^* \tag{7.1}$$

This bound is only practical, however, when the variability of book values is small. Consider a population of $N = 10\,000$ accounts where the total book value is £1 million, and the largest book balance is £1000. Suppose that, in fact, 1% of the accounts contain overstatement errors amounting to £1000, but the auditor has no prior information on this. The prior judgement about the proportion is modelled by the indifference β prior with the parameters $a = 1$ and $b = 1$. Next, a simple random sample of size $n = 100$ is audited, which produces a single error $x = 1$. The amount of error that is found is £15. What is the upper bound B on the total error?

We can use our earlier result that the posterior judgement about the proportion of items in error is also modelled by a β distribution, with revised parameters ($a + x$ and $b + n - x$) in order to identify p^*. For the posterior β distribution $a = 2$ and $b = 100$, the 95th percentile is $p^* = 0.0466$. The auditor is 95% certain that the proportion of accounts in error is no larger than 4.66%. It follows from equation (7.1) that an upper bound on the total error can be calculated:

$$B = 10\,000 \times £1000 \times 0.0466$$

$$B = £466\,000$$

The auditor is at least 95% confident that the total error in the population is less than £466 000.

Considering a single error was discovered in the sample, and that in fact the total error is £1000, this is a distressingly high upper bound.

7.3   Stratified random sampling

The size of the bound B obtained using equation (7.1) is clearly influenced by the amount of the largest account Y_L in the population. Stratified random sampling can substantially tighten the bound by effectively changing this number. Let N_h denote the number of accounts in the hth ($h = 1, \ldots, L$) stratum, Y_{hL} the largest book balance in the hth stratum, and P_h the proportion of accounts in the hth stratum with overstatement errors. A bound for the overstatement error in the hth stratum from equation (7.1) is $B_h = P_h N_h Y_{hL}$. Since the strata are independent, the bound on the overstatement error in the total population is then the sum of the bounds for each stratum: $B = \Sigma B_h = \Sigma P_h N_h Y_{hL}$.

The average number of errors found in each stratum is $n_h P_h$, where n_h is the size of the sample taken from the hth stratum. Now suppose we sample with the total sample size n allocated to each stratum as follows:

$$n_h = \frac{N_h Y_{hL}}{\Sigma N_h Y_{hL}} \cdot n$$

It follows that the average number of errors found in the sample will be the sum of the average errors in each stratum

$$\Sigma n_h P_h = \frac{n}{\Sigma N_h Y_{hL}} \cdot \Sigma N_h Y_{hL} P_h = \frac{n}{\Sigma N_h Y_{hL}} \cdot B$$

The average number of errors in the sample will also be the product of the number sample size n with the overall proportion that are in error:

$$np = \Sigma n_h P_h$$

Using the above result,

$$np = \frac{n}{\Sigma N_h Y_{hL}} \cdot B$$

From which it follows that:

$$B = p \cdot \Sigma N_h Y_{hL} \tag{7.2}$$

An upper bound on the total error is then achieved by choosing as p^* the appropriate percentile of the proportion in error. This is the same method as used in equation (7.1), but with $N \cdot Y_L$ replaced by a smaller amount $\Sigma N_h Y_{hL}$ calculated by stratification.

To illustrate the application of this result, consider the same population as before, but suppose the sample of $n = 100$ was stratified as shown in Table 7.1. Suppose again that the prior proportion in error was modelled as an indifference prior, one error is found in the sample of 100 giving a posterior β distribution whose 95th percentile is $p^* = 0.0466$, as before. Hence a 95% bound on the total error is:

Table 7.1. Values for a stratified sample of $n = 100$.

Book value ($£$)	N_h	Y_{hL} ($£$)	$N_h Y_{hL}$ ($£$)	n_h
1–100	5900	100	590 000	37
101–200	3900	200	780 000	50
201–1000	200	1000	200 000	13
Total	10 000		1 570 000	100

$$B = 0.0466 \times £1\,570\,000 = £74\,481$$

Contrasting this with the bound achieved by simple random sampling from equation (7.1) shows that even limited stratification is effective in tightening the upper confidence bound.

7.4 Monetary unit sampling

To achieve the best results as many strata as possible should be employed. In monetary unit sampling the population is viewed as being composed of Y strata, each containing a sample unit of $£1$, which sums to the population total of $£Y$. Monetary unit sampling (MUS) can be thought of as a limiting situation where stratification by book values yield no further gains since all sample units have the same book value. In order to execute a simple random sampling of money units, each $£1$ should have an equal chance of being selected. Although the sampling unit is the individual pound, rather than an individual invoice or individual balance, the auditor does not verify the individual pound by itself. As Anderson and Teitlebaum[4] explain: 'Rather it acts as a hook and drags a whole account balance with it'. Accordingly, each account is sampled with a chance which increases with its value. If every Jth pound is selected for testing, every account whose value is in excess of $£J$ is automatically tested. (We discuss below how the skip interval J is chosen.) An example of MUS sample selection choosing every 300th pound as the hook is given in Table 7.2.

Account No. 8, with a value of £634 is selected twice (although only tested once) because it is in excess of the skip interval of £300 being used in this example. Having chosen a simple random sample of n pound-units, an upper confidence bound on the total error is obtained by the same equation we used for simple random sampling of accounts except with $Y_L = £1$, and the total population size $N = Y$. Using our earlier example, suppose a random sample of 100 pound-units were selected and tested in such a manner and one overstatement error found, then from equation (7.1)

$$B = 1\,000\,000 \times £1 \times 0.0466$$

$$= £46\,600$$

This confidence bound is even tighter than the one established with stratified sampling.

If the auditor's prior judgement about the proportion of items in error were quantified, then the confidence bound could be tightened further or, alternatively, the same result achieved with a smaller sample size, since prior judgements are equivalent to having already taken a sample.

Table 7.2. Sample selection by choosing every 300th pound as the hook.

Account No.	Account value (£)	Cumulative amount (£)	Individual £ selected	Account selected
1	134	134		
2	18	152		
3	93	245		
4	257	502	300	4
5	155	657	600	5
6	8	665		
7	54	719		
8	634	1353	900,1200	8
9	126	1479		
10	95	1574	1500	10
⋮	⋮	⋮	⋮	⋮

7.5 Sample size and skip interval

If the auditor specifies a monetary precision (MP), or material amount which the total error must not exceed unless a much more rigorous audit will be required, this can be converted into an error proportion as follows:

$$P^* = \frac{MP}{Y}$$

Thus, for illustration, if stocks total £500 000 and they need to be audited to a monetary precision of £30 000 then the error proportion is 6%. The auditor can tolerate some small risk R that the error proportion exceeds p^*. The prior judgement of the auditor will be informed by the inherent risk, that is the chance that material errors occur, and the control risk which is the chance that a material error has not been detected and corrected by the system of internal control. Before any substantive testing is conducted the auditor could quantify the reliance being assigned to internal accounting control:

$$C = \int_0^{p^*} f_\beta(p)\,\mathrm{d}p = \frac{\displaystyle\int_0^{p^*} p^{a-1}(1-p)^{b-1}\mathrm{d}p}{\displaystyle\int_0^1 p^{a-1}(1-p)^{b-1}\mathrm{d}p}$$

where a and b are the parameters of the β prior which models judgement about the proportion of errors. We saw in Chapter 5 that such a prior is equivalent to already having taken a sample of size $(a+b-2)$ of whom $(a-1)$ contained errors. In deciding how large an actual sample size n to test, the auditor needs to achieve the desired reliability R with his posterior β with the parameters $a+x$ and $b+n-x$. That is:

$$R = \frac{\displaystyle\int_0^{p^*} p^{a-1+x}(1-p)^{b+n-x-1}\mathrm{d}p}{\displaystyle\int_0^1 p^{a-1+x}(1-p)^{b+n-x-1}\mathrm{d}p}$$

In order to perform this calculation, the expected number of errors x in a sample size n is also required. If we *assume* that the sample contains zero errors ($x=0$), that the prior is equivalent to a sample of size ($b-1$) containing zero errors (i.e. $a=1$), then the sample size n required to achieve the desired reliability R is found by finding the value of n for which

$$R = \frac{\displaystyle\int_0^{p^*} (1-p)^{n+b-1}\mathrm{d}p}{\displaystyle\int_0^1 (1-p)^{n+b-1}\mathrm{d}p}$$

The solution to this may be found by simple integration, and the result is

$$n+b = \frac{\log(1-R)}{\log(1-p^*)}$$

So when $R = 95\%$ and $p^* = 0.06$, we find that $n+b$ is 49 items. The sample size required, n, is thus $49-b$, where ($b-1$) are the number of items already deemed to have been sampled, derived by quantifying the prior judgement about internal control and other factors. If we attach zero weight to this prior judgement (i.e. ($b-1$) = 0), the required sample size is $n=48$ (or 50 to err on the side of caution). To select n individual pounds from a population of Y pounds, we can take every Jth pound after a random start where $J=Y/n$. In our example of a £500 000 inventory, we would sample every 10 000th pound. This is known as the skip interval for this sampling plan. As we have seen, using this skip interval would result in every stock balance over £10 000 being tested. Monetary unit sampling feels instinctively right—all the very large items in a population are 100% tested, and a sample of the rest are tested, with a greater chance of testing larger items than smaller ones.

7.6 American Institute of Certified Public Accountants audit risk model

The result we obtained in deriving the skip interval ($n+b$) = log ($1-R$)/log($1-p^*$) gives us the linkage between audit risk, R, monetary precision ($p^* = \mathrm{MP}/Y$) and audit evidence. Audit evidence is composed of two sorts: prior judgement about internal controls, b, and judgement based on substantive testing, n. We can reformulate this result into a form more familiar to professional auditors:

$$(n+b) \log(1-p^*) = \log(1-R)$$

$$(1-p^*)^{n+b} = (1-R)$$

$$(1-p^*)^n (1-p^*)^b = (1-R)$$

$$(1-S){\cdot}(1-C) = (1-R)$$

where

$$(1-S) = (1-p^*)^n$$

$$(1-C) = (1-p^*)^b$$

where S is the reliability being derived from substantive tests, C is the reliability being derived from internal accounting control and other relevant factors, and R is the target reliability.

With this notation we have derived the American Institute of Certified Public Accountants (AICPA) model for linking compliance testing with substantive testing:[5]

34. The auditor's judgement concerning the reliance to be assigned to internal accounting control and other relevant factors should determine the reliability level to be used for substantive tests. Such reliability should be set so that the combination of it and the subjective reliance on internal accounting control and other relevant factors will provide a combined reliability level conceptually equal to that which would be used... [when little or no reliance is placed on internal controls]. Thus, the reliability level for substantive tests for particular classes of transactions or balances is not an independent or isolated decision; it is a direct consequence of the auditor's evaluation of internal accounting, and cannot be construed properly out of this context.

35. The concept expressed in paragraph 34, can be applied by use of the following formula:

$$S = 1 - \frac{1-R}{1-C}$$

[This is a rearrangement of $(1-C)(1-S) = (1-R)$.]

This concept is illustrated in the following table, for which the combined reliability level (R) desired is assumed, for illustrative purposes, to be 95%

Auditor's judgement concerning reliance to be assigned to internal accounting control Other relevant Factors. (C)	Resulting reliability level for substantive tests. (S)
90%	50%
70%	83%
50%	90%
30%	93%

The more confidence that an auditor has in internal controls, the less weight needs to be given to substantive testing to achieve the same overall confidence. McRae[6] describes the MUS approach implemented in the early 1960s by the US firm Haskins and Sells, in which field auditors only had to make a choice between three confidence levels to attach to the internal controls. We can use our results to show what the required sample size implied in this scheme would be (see Table 7.3).

Typically, to be 95% confident that MP would be within $p^* = 2\%$ of the total value Y, the sample size should be either 50, 100 or

Table 7.3. The sample size required.

Evaluation of internal controls	Confidence in internal controls, C (%)	Confidence required from substantive test, $S = 1 - \dfrac{(1-R)}{(1-C)}$ (%)	Sample size required,* $n = \dfrac{\log(1-S)}{\log(1-p^*)}$
Very good	86	63	49
Average	63	86	98
Rather poor	0	95	148

Overall reliability $R = 95\%$; MP/$Y = p^* = 0.02$

* $(1-p^*)^n = (1-S)$, hence $n \log(1-p^*) = \log(1-S)$.

150 depending on the degree to which internal controls were to be relied on.

The link we have made between the AICPA risk model, and our approach of quantifying prior judgements as sample equivalents, and then combining this equivalent prior sample with the actual sample is, unfortunately, more tenuous in general. If errors were expected in the sample ($x>0$) or if prior judgement were different ($a>1$) then audit risk cannot be simply broken into two parts: prior judgement based on compliance ($1-C$) and judgement based on vouching ($1-S$). The AICPA risk model is only valid if the components are independent, that is if judgement about the interpretation of evidence from vouching can be made separately from the context of the internal control system from which the evidence is drawn. This is, in general, unlikely to be the case. For a particular illustration consider the sample size needed to achieve a target reliability R, when $a=2$. This is found by finding values of $n+b-1$ which satisfy the equation:

$$R = \frac{\int_0^{p^*} p(1-p)^{n+b-1} \mathrm{d}p}{\int_0^1 p(1-p)^{n+b-1} \mathrm{d}p}$$

Integration by parts gives

$$(1+(b+n)p^*)(1-p^*)^{b+n} = (1-R)$$

and, after taking logs of both sides,

$$b+n = \frac{\log(1-R)}{\log(1-p^*)} - \frac{\log(1+(b+n)p^*)}{\log(1-p)}$$

The earlier result we obtained for zero errors has now acquired an additional term which involves the prior evidence b and the sample evidence n inseparably joined. Audit risk ($1-R$) in this case cannot simply be written as the product of one reliability depending only on substantive testing, n, and another reliability only depending on the prior evidence, b. In general terms, how we evaluate evidence depends on the context, thus, audit risk involves considering substantive testing in the light of prior evidence.

Although the AICPA risk model does need some special

assumptions in order for it to be logically coherent, it does try to communicate an important truth about the combination of judgement and evidence. In terms of the Bayesian model, this communication is obtained at the expense of distorting the logical method for making this combination.

In 1980 the Canadian Institute of Chartered Accountants published the results of a research study 'Extent of Audit Testing' in which judgement and evidence were combined and Bayes' theorem was used. Akresh *et al.*[7] contrast the Canadian model with the AICPA Audit Risk model and set out an agenda of other unresolved issues.

7.7 Combined attributes and variables

In our exposition so far, we have formed bounds by assuming that all overstatement errors are maximum ones. However, when a pound is in error it might be only 1% in error, or 2%, or 3%, and so on up to the maximum 100% overstatement. It is being very conservative indeed to assume that all errors are 100%. The sample when it contains errors gives information on the percentage tainting. The problem of how to combine information on attributes (i.e. whether or not a test item contains an overstatement error) with information on the magnitude of these errors is challenging and has generated several competing proposals in the literature. The original method is known as the Stringer bound, after Kenneth Stringer, a senior executive in Haskins and Sells, who devised the approach. The Stringer[8] bound has proven simple to use, because the required calculations are not difficult, and statistical tables are available. Suppose there are k sample errors, the sample taints $d_i = (y_i - x_i)/y_i$ are calculated and ordered so that $d_1 > d_2 > \ldots > d_k$. The upper confidence bound based on all errors being maximum ones is then reduced by a weighting of these sample taints. The weights associated with the kth taint is:

$$[p^*(k) - p^*(k-1)](1-d_k)$$

where $p^*(k)$ is the $(1-\alpha)100$th percentile of the proportion p when k errors are found in the sample.[9] Earlier we used p^* to denote this percentile without the additional k in brackets;

however, now the taint d_k is associated with the increment in confidence bound from $k-1$ to k errors.

The Stringer method leads to a bound which incorporates information on the taints, and is thus smaller than equation (7.1)

$$B = Y\left[p^*(k) - \sum_{m=1}^{k} [p^*(m) - p^*(m-1)](1-d_m)\right] \quad (7.3)$$

Let us return to the earlier example where a random sample of 100 pound units is selected and one overstatement error of £15 is found. Suppose this overstatement represented 40% of the book value of the account (i.e. $d_1 = 0.4$), then the application of equation (7.3) gives

$$B = 1\,000\,000\left[p^*(1) - [p^*(1) - p^*(0)](1-0.4)\right]$$

Using $p^*(1) = 0.0466$ and $p^*(0) = 0.0295$ leads to $B = 1\,000\,000$ [0.03634] = £36 340.

The bound is now even tighter than the earlier one of £46 600. Nevertheless, as we observed earlier, considering that only a single error was discovered in the sample, and that the total error π_T is only £1000, the Stringer bound is still high. Extensive simulation studies by Leitch et al.,[10] Reneau,[11] and Plante et al.[12] have shown that the Stringer bound is often very much larger than the population total error amount, and that the confidence level always exceeds the specified level. Thus a statement: 'I am at least 95% confident that the total error is less than £36 340' is a highly cautious one.

The Stringer method could be adapted to incorporate something other than an indifference prior ($a=1$, $b=1$), in order to give yet tighter bounds. This, however, is not the approach that appears to be employed in practice, which attempts to incorporate prior information by reducing the confidence level required from the substantive tests using the *ad hoc* AICPA model discussed earlier.

The Stringer method is used in some variant by virtually all large US public accounting firms.[13] The McRae[14] survey of the UK and anecdotal evidence suggest that the use of this method in the UK is much more limited. One can speculate what contextual differences between the UK and USA account for the disparity of interest in this approach.

The Stringer method requires a relatively complex sampling method, i.e. choosing individual pounds rather than physical units. This can require the use of audit software or client assistance to produce a cumulative listing of the population under test. Another problem is that items with zero recorded value are excluded from the sample-selection process. Indeed, understatements pose difficulties for the technique. For example, an item recorded in the books at £10 whose audit value is £2000, gives a sample taint

$$d_i = \text{(book value} - \text{audit value)} / \text{book value}$$

$$= (10 - 2000)/10 = -199.$$

For such large taintings there is no theoretical maximum to their size. A heuristic device is to assume that sample taints never exceed 100%, and perform some non-sampling procedures to check for the reasonableness of this assumption.

The practical importance of the problem of combining attributes and variables, as well as its theoretical challenge, has generated considerable interest among academicians. A number of solutions have been proposed in the accounting literature:

(i)   the multinomial bound devised by Fienberg *et al.*;[2]
(ii)   the cell bound proposed as a variation of the Stringer bound by Leslie *et al.*;[15]
(iii)   the Garstka and Ohlson[16] adjustment to confidence coefficients evaluated by Tamura;[17]
(iv)   the moment bound of Dworin and Grimlund,[18] which is based on an approximation that the posterior distribution can be modelled by a single γ distribution;
(v)   the development of a Bayesian normal bound by Menzefricke and Smieliauskas[19] from the Felix and Grimlund[1] model outlined in Chapter 6;
(vi)   a variation of the bound proposed by Fienberg *et al.*[2] by Tsui *et al.*[20] called the multinomial Dirichlet bound;
(vii)   the modified moment bound of Dworin and Grimlund;[21] and
(viii) the quasi-Bayesian bound due to McCray[3] which is discussed below.

The comparative performance of these alternative methods is

still an active research topic. Plante *et al.*[12] have compared the multinomial, cell and Stringer bounds. Dworin and Grimlund[21] have contrasted their moment bound with McCray's quasi-Bayesian bound.[3] The moment bound has been compared to the multinomial and Stringer bounds by Dworin and Grimlund.[18] Felix *et al.*[22] have reported on a 3-year research and development programme with Arthur Andersen based on an evaluation of these proposals to develop microcomputer subroutines that estimate the smallest appropriate sample sizes and calculate subsequent confidence intervals.

The method of comparison involves simulating a population of account items with known error characteristics (low, medium and high error rates, and understatements and overstatements, with varying size and distribution of errors) and then repeatedly drawing random audit test samples which are evaluated using the competing procedures. Whilst such simulation tests provide evidence of the operating characteristics of the alternative bounds, they are only valid in the context of the particular population being tested and, accordingly, generalizations from this work can be equivocal.

With this qualification the multinomial bound appears uniformly to out-perform the Stringer and the cell bounds, providing tighter bounds at near or above the nominal confidence levels. The multinomial bound out-performs the moment bound only for populations containing large error rates, and overstatement errors. When error rates are small and contain understatements then the moment bound is superior. In tests of the moment bound against the quasi-Bayesian bound neither method uniformly dominates the other.

In the face of such qualified endorsements, an alternative basis for defending an audit judgement is logical consistency. The Stringer, cell and moment bounds, whilst they have the virtue of being easy to compute, are not as consistent with our general approach as is McCray's quasi-Bayesian bound.

7.8 The quasi-Bayesian bound

The method for combining attributes and variables invented by McCray[3] produces a complete posterior distribution of the judgement weights to give to the total amount of error in an accounting population, from quite minimal inputs. The auditor merely has to find the number and size of the taints in an audit sample (or, optionally, any prior judgement about the error can be incorporated), all else follows automatically by calculation. Judgement weights are found by optimization to give the maximum probability of each level of error. Optimization does require the use of a computer; however, the logic of the procedure is relatively straightforward.

The method makes use of the multinomial distribution. In all of this chapter so far we have used the β distribution, which relates to a binary model where observations can only be classified into two categories. The multinomial is a generalization in which observations can fall into many categories C_j, indexed by the subscript j ($j=1, 2, 3, \ldots s$). We further suppose that the sample members have a probability P_j of belonging to category C_j. The probability P_j can be thought of as the proportion of the C_j terms in the population, and

$$\sum_{j=1}^{s} P_j = 1$$

The probability that in a sample of size n, x_1 observations will fall in C_1, x_2 in C_2, and so on

$$\sum_{j=1}^{s} x_j = n$$

is given by

$$P(x_1, x_2, x_3 \ldots, x_s) = \frac{n!}{x_1!\, x_2!\ldots x_s!} P_1^{x_1} P_2^{x_2} \ldots P_s^{x_s}$$

When there are only two categories this reduces to the binomial distribution, since $P_2 = 1-P_1$ and $x_2 = n-x_1$.

We have seen that the binomial model, and its conjugate prior the β distribution, is useful when considering items that can be only 100% in error or 0% in error. However, we have also seen that tainting can be considered as classified as 0% in error, 1% in error, 2% in error and so on up to 100% in error for overstatements and, equally, -1%, -2% and so on down to -100% in error for understatements. If we assume that errors are limited to the range $(-100\%, 100\%)$ and are measured only to the nearest 1%, then there are 201 categories of error.

Just as the binomial is generalized to the multinomial, so the equivalent conjugate β prior is generalized to a Dirichlet distribution

$$f(P_1, P_2, P_3, \ldots, P_s) \propto P_1^{b_1-1} P_2^{b_2-1} \ldots P_s^{b_s-1}$$

A posterior distribution formed by multiplying a prior Dirichlet with a multinomial is also a Dirichlet distribution with b_j+x_j replacing b_j.

Of course, the auditor is only interested in the proportions of different categories of error P_i in the population to the extent that they explain the overall error in the population. That is, if the average taint in the population is

$$D = \sum_{i=-100}^{100} d_i P_i$$

where P_i is the proportion of category i and d_i is the taint of category $i [d_i = i/100]$, the total error π_T in the population will be

$$YD = \pi_T$$

From this it follows that an auditor's judgement about the total error in the population $f(\pi_T)$ can be based on a judgement about the average taint in the population $f(D)$, which in turn depends on beliefs about the individual proportions P_i of the different categories of taint. To expect an auditor to quantify his judgement about 201 categories of taint is somewhat unrealistic. Fortunately, McCray's model does not require the auditor to individually quantify his belief about 201 proportions of error, rather the *worst* proportions are calculated which give the highest probability to each type of error. That is, for a particular value of the total error, values of P_i are chosen to maximize the Dirichlet posterior:

maximise
$$L(\pi_{\mathrm{T}}) = K \prod_{i=-100}^{100} P_i^{b_i + x_i - 1}$$

subject to

$$Y \sum_{i=-100}^{100} d_i P_i = \pi_{\mathrm{T}}$$

and

$$\sum_{i=-100}^{100} P_i = 1$$

and $0 \le P_i \le 1$, where K is a constant of proportionality (the multinomial coefficient). This is a non-linear optimization problem with inequality constraints. McCray's program uses one of the optimizing algorithms developed by P. Wolfe of the IBM Research Institute to solve such problems.[23]

7.9 Numerical illustration

Let us assume an indifference prior (i.e. $b_i = 1$ for all proportions). A monetary unit sample of 100 items is drawn from a population of accounts totalling £1 000 000. Two errors are found: 30% and 40% overstatement taintings. To calculate the worst proportion of such taintings in the whole population we find values of P_{30}, P_{40}, P_0 and P_{100} which have the highest probability of occurring. That is we maximize the multinomial probability

$$L(\pi_{\mathrm{T}}) = \frac{100!}{98!} P_0 P_{40}^{98} P_{30}$$

such that the proportions sum to one

$$P_0 + P_{30} + P_{40} + P_{100} = 1$$

such that the average taint gives the total error $1\,000\,000\,\{0P_0 + 0.3P_{30} + 0.4P_{40} + 1P_{100}\} = \pi_{\mathrm{T}}$ and that all proportions are non-negative and less than one.

If we choose a total error of size $\pi_{\mathrm{T}i} = 33\,000$ then the proportions which would give the highest probability to an error of this magnitude using the optimization algorithm are

$$P_0 = 0.94766$$

$$P_{100} = 0.02241$$

$$P_{30} = 0.01381$$

$$P_{40} = 0.01612$$

The likelihood or probability of such an error $L(\pi_{Ti}) = L(33\,000) = 0.0114$. For such a value of the total error π_{Ti} we can similarly compute the maximum likelihood and the underlying proportions of taints. The results of this computation for each total error π_{Ti} from £1000 to £33 000 are listed in Table 7.4.

Having calculated the maximum likelihoods for a range of errors, the next step is to compute the posterior probabilities, i.e. how much judgement weight should be given to each value of error. In McCray's quasi-Bayesian model, this set of maximum likelihoods (technically a profile likelihood) is treated as if it were an ordinary likelihood which can be rescaled by using Bayes' theorem to give the required posterior distribution. Since

Table 7.4. The maximum likelihood for total error.*

Total error, π_{Ti}	Maximum likelihood, $L(\pi_{Ti})$	Proportion of taints (%)			
		0	100	30	40
1000	0.0155	0.99709	—	0.00163	0.00128
2000	0.0466	0.99420	—	0.00320	0.00260
3000	0.0787	0.99133	—	0.00469	0.00398
4000	0.1052	0.98847	—	0.00612	0.00541
5000	0.1235	0.98563	—	0.00748	0.00689
6000	0.1337	0.98281	—	0.00877	0.00842
7000	0.1367	0.98000	—	0.01000	0.01000
8000	0.1342	0.97721	—	0.01116	0.01163
9000	0.1276	0.97443	—	0.01227	0.01330
10000	0.1184	0.97167	—	0.01331	0.01502
11000	0.1077	0.96922	0.00017	0.01413	0.01648
⋮	⋮	⋮	⋮	⋮	⋮
32000	0.0126	0.94864	0.02140	0.01383	0.01613
33000	0.0114	0.94766	0.02241	0.01381	0.01612

* From McCray.[3]

we have assumed a uniform prior, the rescaling constant is the sum of the likelihoods, i.e.

$$f(\pi_{Ti}) = \frac{L(\pi_{Ti})}{\sum\limits_{j=1}^{201} L(\pi_{Tj})}$$

In general, if the auditor quantified prior judgement weights for the total error $P(\pi_{Ti})$, then the posterior judgement would be proportional to this prior times the likelihood, i.e.

$$f(\pi_{Ti}) = \frac{P(\pi_{Ti}) \times L(\pi_{Ti})}{\sum\limits_{j=1}^{201} P(\pi_{Tj}) \times L(\pi_{Tj})}$$

To complete the illustration, the sum of the likelihoods is 2.12935, hence the posterior weights are found by dividing each likelihood by this amount (see Table 7.5 and Figure 7.1).

7.10 A diagrammatic illustration

McCray's model[3] for evaluating dollar unit samples is a considerable achievement. It generates a posterior distribution on the expected total error in an accounting population from minimal inputs. Such a weight function provides the basis for defensible judgements about the magnitudes of error that could be found. It can deal with both errors of understatement and errors of overstatement in the sample. It can incorporate prior beliefs about error proportions, or present acceptable evaluations in the absence of any informative prior. The calculations required cannot easily be performed by hand. In this section we explain diagrammatically what the calculations are, and why a computer is needed. For ease of exposition an indifference or ignorance prior is assumed. We also, for reasons that will become clear, stick to a simple problem of evaluating a sample with only one error type. Our illustration has much in common with how linear programming is commonly presented. We discuss a simple form which can be drawn in two dimensions, and then rely on the reader's imagination to consider how the problem would look in more dimensions.

Assume a MUS sample of size n is taken and a single taint d is found, and there are $(n-1)$ error free items. In the whole

Error	Probability from 0.0 to 0.0642 by 0.00128	Individual	Cumulative
1000.0		0.0073	0.007
2000.0		0.0219	0.029
3000.0		0.0370	0.066
4000.0		0.0494	0.116
5000.0		0.0580	0.174
6000.0		0.0628	0.236
7000.0		0.0642	0.301
8000.0		0.0630	0.364
9000.0		0.0599	0.423
10000.0		0.0556	0.479
11000.0		0.0506	0.530
12000.0		0.0457	0.575
13000.0		0.0413	0.617
14000.0		0.0373	0.654
15000.0		0.0337	0.688
16000.0		0.0305	0.718
17000.0		0.0275	0.746
18000.0		0.0249	0.771
19000.0		0.0224	0.793
20000.0		0.0203	0.813
21000.0		0.0183	0.832
22000.0		0.0165	0.848
23000.0		0.0149	0.863
24000.0		0.0135	0.876
25000.0		0.0122	0.889
26000.0		0.0110	0.900
27000.0		0.0099	0.910
28000.0		0.0089	0.918
29000.0		0.0081	0.926
30000.0		0.0073	0.934
31000.0		0.0066	0.940
32000.0		0.0059	0.946
33000.0		0.0053	0.952
34000.0		0.0048	0.956
35000.0		0.0043	0.961
36000.0		0.0039	0.965
37000.0		0.0035	0.968
38000.0		0.0032	0.971
39000.0		0.0029	0.974
40000.0		0.0026	0.977
41000.0		0.0023	0.979
42000.0		0.0021	0.981
43000.0		0.0019	0.983
44000.0		0.0017	0.985
45000.0		0.0015	0.986
46000.0		0.0014	0.988
47000.0		0.0012	0.989
48000.0		0.0011	0.990
49000.0		0.0010	0.991
50000.0		0.0009	0.992
51000.0		0.0008	0.993
52000.0		0.0007	0.993
53000.0		0.0007	0.994

Figure 7.1. Partial graph of the posterior probabilities from the example given in the text.

population, P_0 is the proportion of items with zero taint and P_d is the proportion of items with taint size d. If the greatest taint possible in the population is 100% then the average taint will be at least

$$0P_0 + dP_d + 1P_{100} = D$$

Table 7.5. Maximum likelihoods, posterior and cumulative posterior probabilities for the proposed model for states of nature from the example given in the text.*

State of nature	Maximum likelihood†	Posterior probabilities‡	Cumulative probabilities
0	0.0000§	0.00000	0.0000***
1000	0.0155	0.00728	0.0073
2000	0.0466	0.02187	0.0292
2564‖			0.0500
3000	0.0787	0.03698	0.0661
4000	0.1052	0.04940	0.1155
5000	0.1235	0.05801	0.1735
6000	0.1337	0.06277	0.2363
7000	0.1367	0.06420	0.3005
8000	0.1342	0.06302	0.3635
9000	0.1276	0.05993	0.4235
10000	0.1184	0.05561	0.4791
11000	0.1077	0.05073	0.5296
.	.	.	.
.	.	.	.
.	.	.	.
32000	0.0126	0.00591	0.9462
32707‖			0.9500
33000	0.0114	0.00533	0.9515
.	.	.	.
.	.	.	.

* Sample size 100; reported book value \$1 000 000; percentage overstatement taintings 30 and 40; uniform prior distribution assumed 95% upper bound \$32 707, and 5% lower bound \$2564; posterior expectation 13 603; posterior variance 0.982699×10^8; sum of maximum likelihoods 2.12935.

† $L(\pi_{Ti})$ see Table 7.4 for the underlying proportions for the maximum likelihoods.

‡ Col (2)/2.12935.

§ Since in the example the only taintings assumed are 100% overstatement and those found in the sample.

‖ Assumes straight-line interpolation.

Now, by definition, the proportion of each error type must sum to one, i.e.

$$P_0 + P_d + P_{100} = 1$$

By substituting for P_{100}, we may represent the average taint in P_d and P_0 terms only:

$$dP_d + (1 - P_0 - P_d) = D$$
$$P_0 + (1-d)P_d = (1-D)$$

For a given value of D this equation gives all the combinations of P_0 and P_d which could underlie it. The proportions P_0 and P_d also give the probability of observing the sample result. The likelihood of obtaining only one error in a sample size n depends only on P_0 and P_d:

$$L(\pi_{Ti}) = KP_0^{n-1}P_d$$

The likelihood as a function of P_0 and P_d is shown graphically in Figure 7.2. The curves L_1, L_2 and L_3 are isoquants, that is the contours of the likelihood function of equal value. Just as on a two-dimensional map, hills and valleys may be represented by contours, so Figure 7.2 uses steeper curves to show higher values of likelihood. The values of P_0 and P_d which underlie a given value of D are chosen such that they maximize this likelihood.

The process for small values of D is represented in Figure 7.3. The line $A_1B_1C_1$ gives the combinations of P_0 and P_d which satisfy the equation $P_0 + (1-d)P_d = (1-D)$ and is superimposed on the likelihood curves. The point B_1 gives values (P_0, P_d) for which the likelihood reaches a maximum value. The line $A_2B_2C_2$ gives the combinations of P_0 and P_d for a different value of D.

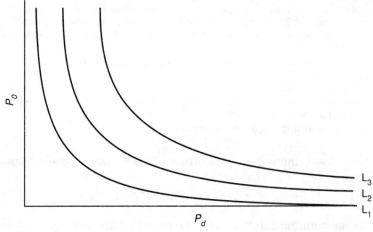

Figure 7.2. Plot of likelihood isoquants versus P_0 and P_d.

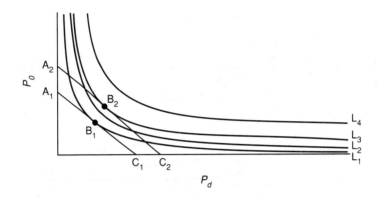

Figure 7.3. Maximum likelihoods for small values of error.

For each value that D can take (0%, 1%, 2%...) there will be a line parallel to $A_1B_1C_1$, and a new maximum value of the likelihood. The McCray quasi-Bayesian model steps through the amounts that D can take in order to compute a likelihood value for each value of D. It is these likelihood values which in turn are rescaled so that they form a coherent posterior weight function for beliefs to attach the values of D (and thence to the values of the total error YD). In this way the auditor does not have to form a judgement about the proportion of each error type P_0, P_d (which in the full model comes to 201 types of taint).

The calculations for larger values of D are more involved because a second constraint comes into play, namely $P_0 + P_d + P_{100} = 1$, or $P_0 + P_d \leqslant 1$ (treating P_{100} as a slack variable). This constraint is shown as the line EF in Figure 7.4. The effect of this is that the maximum value of the likelihood no longer automatically occurs when the likelihood curve is a tangent to the line (as is B_1), but can occur at points such as B_2 and B_3 where the two constraints intersect.

The McCray model then produces a curious track through the contours of the likelihood function. For low values of $(1-D)$, or large values of D, tangential points are selected, for higher values of $(1-D)$ points of intersection are selected. This calculation can be represented in two dimensions when only one error type is found; however, when several error types occur the multinomial likelihood cannot be simply drawn as isoquants. This is the point

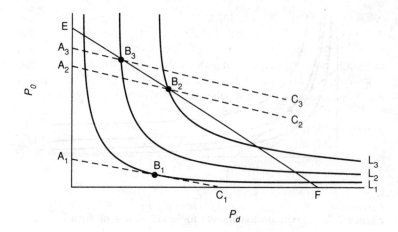

Figure 7.4. Maximum likelihoods for large values of error.

of departure from flat sheets of paper, to the world of n dimensions and intersecting hyperplanes that are tangential to convex spaces. Fortunately, such worlds exist inside computers, and the method we have described for a simple problem works for the more complex situation.

7.11 Two simple cases of the quasi-Bayesian bound

Having explained why, in general, a computer is needed to perform the optimization routines required to use a quasi-Bayesian bound, there are two simple cases which can be solved by hand:

(i)   when there is no error in a monetary unit sample; and
(ii) when there is a single error in a monetary unit sample.

These special cases allow us to see the McCray computations. More intriguingly, these two cases allow us to complete a circle, drawing together our earlier discussion of modelling judgement about proportions of an attribute in a population using a β distribution, with our present concern of judgements about magnitudes of variables such as sizes of error in a population. In these two simple cases we find that the quasi-Bayesian bound reduces to a simple formula for judgement weights. This simple formula turns out to be a β distribution! The same technique for modelling judgement about the proportion of items in error, provides us with a means of evaluating a monetary unit sample.

Consider a MUS of 100 items, which has been tested and in which no errors have been discovered. We assume that we have zero prior information, and we wish to put a bound on the judgement weight we ought to attach to the errors we have failed to discover. There are a range of values for the average tainting D in the population, and the task is to put the worst light we can on each value of D, which is consistent with the evidence. If we assume that all undiscovered taints are 100% in error (i.e. conservative assumption), then the average taint D will be defined by the untainted proportion P_0 and the tainted proportion P_{100} in the population. That is $D = 0P_0 + 1P_{100} = P_{100}$.

In addition, since we only have two categories of taint to consider, it follows that

$$P_0 + P_{100} = 1$$

If the population value is $Y = \pounds 1\,000\,000$, then the judgement weights to be put on the undiscovered errors in the population π_T correspond to the judgement weight put on each value of D since $\pi_T = DY$.

The steps required to obtain a judgement weight for the average taint D rely on Bayes' theorem that posterior judgement is proportional to the prior multiplied by the likelihood. With a uniform prior judgement, the posterior judgement is shaped entirely by the likelihood of the evidence. We need to calculate the likelihood of the evidence that corresponds to various values of D. In order to give the greatest judgement weight to the values of D, we maximize the likelihood. Thus our judgement weight is formed in a two-step fashion.

(i) For a range of values D, e.g. 0%, 1%, 2%, ..., 100%, we maximize

$$L(\pi_T) = YL(D)$$

where $L(D)$ is the likelihood of D and

$$L(D) = K\,P_0^{100}$$

where K is a proportionality coefficient, subject to

$$P_0 + P_{100} = 1$$

and also subject to

$$P_{100} = D$$

and

$$0 \leqslant P_0, P_{100} \leqslant 1$$

(ii) We calculate the posterior judgement $L(\pi_{\mathrm{T}})$ by rescaling $L(D)$ so that it allocates 100% probability weight across the categories. In a simple example of zero errors, we can convert a constrained maximization problem into an unconstrained one by using the constraint to substitute for P_0:

$$L(D) = K(1-D)^{100}$$

In performing the calculations the proportionality coefficient K is set equal to unity, since we will be rescaling. Furthermore, for values of $D > 10\%$, $L(D)$ becomes miniscule, thus we calculate over a smaller range of taints: 0% to 10%. The results are shown in Table 7.6. For each error we have calculated a bound on the judgement weight that we should attach. The weight that the

Table 7.6. The quasi-Bayesian bound for zero errors in a monetary unit sample of size 100.

State of nature, D (%)	State of nature, YD (£)	Maximum likelihood, $L(D)$	Posterior probability*
0	0	1.000000	0.636091
1	10 000	0.366033	0.232830
2	20 000	0.132620	0.084358
3	30 000	0.047552	0.030247
4	40 000	0.016870	0.010731
5	50 000	0.005920	0.003765
6	60 000	0.002054	0.001307
7	70 000	0.000705	0.000448
8	80 000	0.000239	0.000152
9	90 000	0.000080	0.000051
10	100 000	0.000026	0.000016
Sum $L(D)$		1.572102	

* Rescaled by division by 1.572102.

error exceeds £80 000 is no more than $(0.000152 + 0.000051 + 0.000016 = 0.000219)$ or 0.02%. The judgement weight we have given to each value of D was calculated as $K(1-D)^{100}$. In general, if our sample size were $(b-1)$, then the judgement weight would be $K(1-D)^{b-1}$.

If D were continuous, taking any value in the range (0, 100%), then we would recognize that judgement weights as being allocated by the quasi-Bayesian bound used a β distribution over D with the parameters $a=1$ and $b=b$. The quasi-Bayesian bound in the case of zero errors operates as a discrete version of a β distribution. In the zero error case, one evaluates an MUS sample using a beta distribution!

Let us take a second case of a MUS, this time with a sample size of 100 and a single error of size d. Let us assume first that the error size d is a 100% taint. We find that $P_0 + P_{100} = 1$ and $P_{100} = D$. The unconstrained optimization problem is to maximize $L(D) = K(1-D)^{99}D$, which is computed as before. The results of this procedure are given in Table 7.7.

In this case the weight of judgement that the error exceeds £80 000 is increased to $(0.002284 + 0.000871 + 0.000324 =$

Table 7.7. The quasi-Bayesian bound for a single 100% taint in a monetary unit sample of size 100.

State of nature, D (%)	State of nature, YD (£)	Maximum likelihood, $L(D)$	Posterior probability*
0	0	0	0.000000
1	10 000	0.003697	0.406074
2	20 000	0.002706	0.297257
3	30 000	0.001471	0.161526
4	40 000	0.000703	0.077202
5	50 000	0.000312	0.034223
6	60 000	0.000131	0.014405
7	70 000	0.000053	0.005829
8	80 000	0.000020	0.002284
9	90 000	0.000008	0.000871
10	100 000	0.000003	0.000324
Sum $L(D)$		0.009104	

* Rescaled by division by 0.009104.

0.003479) or 0.3%. Again we can identify the weight function being used in the quasi-Bayesian bound as a β distribution on D with the parameters $a=2$ and $b=100$. This has a mean at $2/102 = 0.0196$, giving a mean error in the population of £19 600. In both of these simple cases the β distribution appears as the model for judgement weights. For completeness, now consider a sample in which the single error is found of size d (less than 100%), the constrained optimization problem is to maximize

$$L(D) = KP_0^{n-1} P_d$$

subject to

$$P_0 + P_d + P_{100} = 1$$

$$dP_d + P_{100} = D$$

where $0 \leqslant P_0, P_d, P_{100} \leqslant 1$.

Using the constraints gives $P_{100} = D - dP_d$, whence

$$P_0 + P_d + D - dP_d = 1$$

to give

$$P_d = \frac{1}{(1-d)} [1 - D - P_0]$$

Since $0 \leqslant P_d$, this substitution is only valid for values $P_0 \leqslant 1-D$. That is, in maximizing the likelihood (as we saw with the diagrammatic exposition shown in Figure 7.4) one has to ensure that the function remains within the feasible region. However, for *small values* of D we can treat P_{100} as a slack variable, and get the constraints

$$P_0 + P_d \leqslant 1$$

and

$$dP_d \leqslant D$$

For small values of D the maximum of the likelihood occurs at the boundary of the feasible region, where these two constraints intersect, i.e.

$$P_d = D/d$$

and

$$P_d = 1 - P_0$$

From this it follows that the likelihood being maximized is

$$L(D) = K \left(1 - \frac{D}{d}\right)^{99} \frac{D}{d}$$

This we identify as a β distribution on D/d, with the parameters $a=2$ and $b=100$. The effect of the sample taint not being 100% is to increase the likelihood of lower values of D.

For *large values* of D, we saw that points of tangency are chosen, giving the maximum of the likelihood inside the feasible region of P_0, P_d, P_{100} and not at the boundary. To address the maximization of likelihood for large values of D, substitute

$$P_d = \frac{1}{(1-d)} [(1-D)-P_0]$$

and then the likelihood to be maximized is

$$L(D) = K P_0^{99} \frac{1}{(1-d)} [1-D-P_0]$$

The value of P_0 to maximize this function is found where the gradient is flat, or the first derivative is zero:

$$\frac{\partial L(D)}{\partial P_0} = K \frac{1}{(1-d)} [(1-D) 99 P_0^{98} - 100 P_0^{99}] = 0$$

The value $P_0 = (99/100) (1-D)$ is the result we require. (Checking that the second derivative is negative at this point confirms that we have a value of P_0 which maximizes the likelihood.) The maximum value of the likelihood corresponding to each level of taint can now be expressed as

$$L(D) = K \frac{1}{(1-d)} (0.99)^{99} (1-D)^{99} \left(1-D-0.99 (1-D)\right)$$

$$= K \frac{1}{(1-d)} \frac{1}{100} (0.99)^{99} (1-D)^{100}$$

This is a β distribution on D with the parameters $a=1$ and $b=100$. The treatment of a single error of taint size d in the sample requires a mixture of two β distributions:

$$L(D) = K\left(1 - \frac{D}{d}\right)^{99}\frac{D}{d} \qquad (7.4)$$

and

$$L(D) = K\frac{1}{(1-d)}\frac{1}{100}(0.99)^{99}(1-D)^{100} \qquad (7.5)$$

The switch over occurs when the value of P_0 changes from being at the boundary, such as point B_2 in Figure 7.4, to the interior maximum likelihood estimate point B_1. The point of transition is when $(99/100)(1-D) = 1-(D/d)$ or $D = d/(100-99d)$.

For small values of D (less than $d/(100-99d)$) the judgement weight is calculated using equation (7.4). This has a non-zero mode, $(a=2, b=100)$, which occurs when $D = 0.01d$. The larger the sample taint value d, the more values of D there are that satisfy the condition of being less than $d/(100-99d)$, and the more of the judgement weight is calculated using equation (7.4). When values of D no longer satisfy this condition, judgement weight switches to being calculated using equation (7.5). The solution is shown graphically in Figure 7.5, showing that the right-hand tail of the quasi-Bayesian bound in the case of a single error is a β distribution with $a=1$.

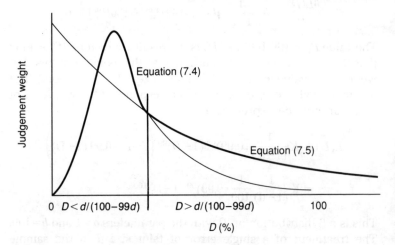

Figure 7.5. A mixture of two β distributions.

The results of the computation of a quasi-Bayesian bound for a single 40% taint in a MUS sample of size 100 are given in Table 7.8. The weight of the judgement that the undiscovered errors in the population exceed £80 000 is (0.00041 + 0.00014 + 0.00004 = 0.00059) or 0.06%. This is three times larger than the result for a MUS sample with zero errors, but five times smaller than when the single error in the MUS sample was 100% tainted. In Section 7.7 the 95% Stringer bound for a single 40% overstatement in a MUS sample of 100 was calculated as £36 340. The equivalent quasi-Bayesian bound from Table 7.8 would be £30 000 (0.63980 + 0.23181 + 0.08311 = 0.95742, or 95%).

7.12 Summary

In this chapter we have brought the interface between theory and practice even closer. We have addressed a key audit problem of forming defensible judgements about accounting populations tainted with rare errors. The neglected steps of risk estimation and risk evaluation have been made explicit. Where these

Table 7.8. The quasi-Bayesian bound for a single 40% taint in a monetary unit sample of size 100.

State of nature, D (%)	State of nature, YD (£)	Maximum likelihood, $L(D)$	Posterior probability*
0	0	0.000000	0
1	10 000	0.002706	0.63980
2	20 000	0.000980	0.23181
3	30 000	0.000351	0.08311
4	40 000	0.000125	0.02948
5	50 000	0.000043	0.01034
6	60 000	0.000015	0.00359
7	70 000	0.000005	0.00123
8	80 000	0.000001	0.00041
9	90 000	0.000000	0.00014
10	100 000	0.000000	0.00004
Sum $L(D)$		0.004230	

* Rescaled by division by 0.004230.

processes remain implicit, the auditor, his field staff and his students are prey to inappropriate biases in the treatment of evidence, from failing to extract sufficient meaning from the evidence and not revising judgement sufficiently, to the other extreme of over-reacting to evidence and assuming that it is much more reliable than prior judgement. The gleeful investigation of the common failures in audit judgement is a topical and active research question. Development has reached such a level that student training exercises are now available to demonstrate common fallacies in audit judgement.[24] For our key problem of making judgements about rare errors a prevalent mistake in audit practice has only recently been discovered. This is to identify certain errors as 'unique' and consequently to omit them from the projection of total error in the audit population. This practice leads to auditors systematically to underestimate population error and their β risk in accepting management's assertion. Burgstahler and Jiambalvo[25] have described this practice with an illustration:

> Suppose an auditor is evaluating a sample of customer accounts and finds an error resulting from a temporary clerical employee misfooting an invoice. Although normal procedures call for clerks to foot invoices twice to ensure accuracy, the temporary employee did not follow procedures. A 100 per cent examination of the invoices prepared by the temporary worker turns up two additional errors which are corrected. Further observation and discussion with client personnel indicates that other employees always check footings of invoices. Thus, the auditor has determined that it is very unlikely that similar undiscovered errors exist.

The issue is: How should such an error be treated? How should judgement be revised? Using the automatic computation of error bounds approach the reason for the error is not a relevant piece of information in deciding how judgement should be changed. All errors are treated consistently. What Burgstahler and Jiambalvo suggest is that, in practice:

> when the discovered error appears to be relatively dissimilar to other errors in the category, auditors ... may not consider the observation as indicative of errors in the population. Therefore, the auditor may consider projection of the error unwarranted and 'isolate' the error.

Casual empiricism suggests that this practice is widespread in the UK. The fallacy in this approach is that, whilst the auditor may be sure that there are no *identical* errors in the population, there may be *other unique* errors; that is different errors which are also unique. Properly evaluated, the sample gives evidence about the magnitude and incidence of these other undiscovered but 'unique' errors.

The intellectual challenge of auditing is to form a judgement about what has not been found, for this reason errors should not be 'isolated'. Since every discovered audit error will have some unique characteristic, with a little imagination every follow-up investigation could lead to most errors being isolated. Pursuing such a policy would lead to judgements which systematically underestimate the total errors and the risk. The quasi-Bayesian MUS approach we have described here would more prudently quantify judgement and permit a logical and defensible assessment of risk.

As our exposition has indicated, some things remain to be done before the approach we have described makes its transition from academic blackboards and journals into standard operating procedures for the industry. Much has been achieved in classroom and research settings. Effective implementation would need to proceed on two fronts. First, the conversion of the prototypes into robust decision-support tools which would help structure, organize and guide the auditor through the complexity of judgements about audit risk and audit evidence. The second front would be to develop educational programmes, examination syllabuses and training courses which would expound the thinking embedded in these formal models of audit judgement, teaching students how to use the tools, improving their efficiency, their quality, their ability to understand and hence adapt to change and, hopefully, their job satisfaction.

Notes and references

1   W.L. Felix and R.A. Grimlund (1977) A sampling model for audit tests of composite accounts, *Journal of Accounting Research*, **Spring**, 23–41.
2   S.E. Fienberg, J. Neter and R.A. Leitch (1977) Estimating the total overstatement error in accounting populations, *Journal of the American Statistical Association*, **Jun.**, 295–302.

3   J.H. McCray (1984) A quasi-Bayesian audit risk model for dollar unit sampling, *The Accounting Review*, **Jan.**, 35–51.
4   D. Anderson and A. Teitlebaum (1973) Dollar unit sampling, *Canadian Chartered Accountant*, **102**(4), 30–39.
5   American Institute of Certified Public Accountants, *Statements on Auditing Standards, Codification of Auditing Standards and Procedures*, AICPA, 1 July 1978, Section 320B.35. Discussed in: A.D. Bailey (1981) *Statistical Auditing: Review, Concepts and Problems*, London: Harcourt Brace Jovanovich.
6   T.W. McCrae (1974) *Statistical Sampling for Audit and Control*, p. 202. New York: Wiley.
7   A.P. Akresh, J.L. Loebbecke and W.R. Scott (1988) Audit approaches and techniques. In: A.R. Abdel-Khalik and I. Solomon (Eds). *Research Opportunities in Auditing: The Second Decade*, pp. 20–23. Sarasota, FL: American Accounting Association.
8   K.W. Stringer (1963) Practical aspects of statistical sampling in auditing, in *Proceedings of The Business and Economic Statistics Section, 1963*, pp. 405–411. Washington DC: American Statistical Association.
9   Stringer used a Poisson approximation to obtain $p^*(k)$ the $(1-\alpha)$100th percentile of the proportion p when k errors are found in a sample of size n. That is

$$\frac{\int_0^{p^*(k)} p^k (1-p)^{n-k} \mathrm{d}p}{\int_0^1 p^k (1-p)^{n-k} \, \mathrm{d}p} \approx \frac{(np^*(k))^k}{k!} \exp\left(-np^*(k)\right)$$

So, for illustration, if there is a single error $k=1$ in a sample of size $n=100$, the 95th percentile is the value of $p^*(1)$ for which $100p^*(1) \exp\left(-100p^*(1)\right) = (1-0.95)$. Trial and error shows that the value of $p^*(1)$ which satisfies this equation is $p^*(1) = 0.0466$.
10   R.A. Leitch, J. Neter, R. Plante and P. Sinha (1982) Modified multinomial bounds for larger numbers of errors in audits, *The Accounting Review*, **Apr.**, 384–400.
11   J.H. Reneau (1978) CAV bounds in dollar unit sampling: some simulation results, *The Accounting Review*, **Jul.**, 669–680.
12   R. Plante, J. Neter and R.A. Leitch (1985) Comparative performance of multinomial, cell and Stringer bounds, *Auditing: A Journal of Practice and Theory*, **Autumn**, 40–56.
13   R.A. Grimlund and M.S. Schroeder (1988) On the current use of the Stringer method of MUS: some new directions, *Auditing: A Journal of Practice and Theory*, **8**(1), 53–62.
14   T.W. McRae (1982) *A Study of the Application of Statistical Sampling to External Auditing*. London: Institute of Chartered Accountants in England and Wales.
15   D.A. Leslie, A. Teitlebaum and D. Anderson (1979) *Dollar Unit*

Sampling—A Practical Guide for Auditors. Belmont, CA: Fearon-Pitman Publishers.

16 S.J. Garstka and P.A. Ohlson (1979) Ratio estimation in accounting populations with probabilities of sample section proportional to size of book values, *Journal of Accounting Research*, **Autumn**, 179–192.

17 H. Tamura (1985) Analysis of the Garstka–Ohlson Bounds, *Auditing: A Journal of Practice and Theory*, **4**(2), 133–142.

18 L. Dworin and R.A. Grimlund (1984) Dollar unit sampling for accounts receivable and inventory, *The Accounting Review*, **Apr.**, 218–241.

19 M. Menzefricke and W. Smieliauskas (1984) A simulation study of the performance of parametric dollar unit sampling statistical procedures, *Journal of Accounting Research*, **Autumn**, 588–604.

20 K.W. Tsui, E.M. Matsumura and K.L. Tsui (1985) Multinomial-Dirichlet bounds for dollar-unit sampling in auditing, *The Accounting Review*, **Jan.**, 79–96.

21 L. Dworin and R.A. Grimlund (1986) Dollar unit sampling: a comparison of quasi Bayesian and moment bounds, *The Accounting Review*, **Jan.**, 36–57.

22 W.L. Felix, R.A. Grimlund, F.J. Koster and R.S. Roussey (1990) Arthur Andersen's new monetary unit sampling approach, *Auditing: A Journal of Practice and Theory*, **9**(3), 1–16.

23 McCray (see note 3) uses different notation to that which we have employed. The model is set out in the original paper as:

$$L(\theta) = \text{maximum } K \prod_{i=-100}^{100} (a_i + p_i)^{n_i}$$

$$\sum_{i=-100}^{100} (a_i + p_i) = 1$$

$$\frac{\text{RBV}}{100} \sum_{i=-100}^{100} i(a_i + p_i) = \theta$$

$$0 \leq a_i, p_i \leq 1$$

The identification $\theta \equiv \pi_{\text{T}}$, RBV $= Y$, $i/100 = d_i$, $n_i = x_i$. The a_i relate to the prior proportions of taints, which McCray does not confine to coming from a conjugate prior, but could be derived from any prior. The relationship between the original formulation and that set out here is

$$(a_i + p_i)^{ni} = p_i^{b_i + n_i - 1}$$

The general Bayesian risk model (GBRM) program is a research code available from John J. McCray, The College of William and Mary, Williamsburg, Virginia 23185, USA.

24   See: R.H. Ashton (1984) Integrating research and teaching in auditing:
      Fifteen cases on judgement and decision making, *The Accounting
      Review*, **Jan.**, 78–97.
25   D. Burgstahler and J. Jiambalvo (1986) Sample error characteristics
      and projection of error to audit populations, *The Accounting Review*,
      Apr., 233–248.
26   R.A. Grimlund (1988) Sample size planning for the moment method
      of MUS: incorporating audit judgements, *Auditing: A Journal of
      Practice and Theory*, **2**, 77–104.
27   E.J. Blocker and J. Robertson (1976) Bayesian sampling procedures
      for auditing computer-assisted instruction, *The Accounting Review*,
      359–363.
28   M.J. Abdolmohammadi (1987) Decision Support and Export Systems
      in Auditing: A Review and Research Directions, *Accounting and
      Business Research*, **Spring**, 173–185.
29   E.J. Blocher (1985) A computer assisted teaching aid for Bayesian
      audit sampling, *Advances in Accounting*, **2**, 113–148.
30   M.E. Novick and P.H. Jackson (1974) *Statistical Methods for
      Educational and Psychological Research*, McGraw-Hill, New York.
31   W.R. Kinney (1983) A note on compounding probabilities in auditing,
      Auditing: A Journal of Practice and Theory, **Spring**, 13–22.

APPENDIX 7.1
Computer programs and research codes for Bayesian methods in statistical auditing

Program	General Bayesian risk model for multiple populations
Synopsis	The software computes a probability distribution on the total error in an accounting population using the quasi-Bayesian model as described in McCray.[3]
Use requirements	IBM PC with mathematics co-processor chip (8087). Supplied in FORTRAN Source and a compiled version.
Contact	Professor John H. McCray, School of Business Administration, The College of William and Mary, Williamsburg, Virginia 23185, USA. Tel. (804) 253 4611

Program	Sample size planning
Synopsis	Research codes for sample size planning and calculation of confidence bounds based on methods of moments (see Felix *et al.*[22] and Grimlund[26]). Available at nominal duplicating cost for not-for-profit educational use and for experimental use in other organizations.
Contact	Richard A. Grimlund, Department of Accounting, College of Business Administration, University of Iowa, Iowa City, IA 52242, USA.

Program	Bayesian audit sampling—attributes
Synopsis	The software computes a risk level for a Bayesian attributes sample, given prior probabilities and sample results (see Blocker and Robertson[27]).
Use requirements	IBM PC or PC Compatible; IBM Basic or Compatible Basic.
Contact	Edward J. Blocher, Professor of Accounting, Accounting Faculty, School of Business, University of North Carolina, Chapel Hill, North Carolina 27599, USA. Tel. 919-962-3200.

Program	Bayesian assisted sampling system (BASS)
Synopsis	BASS uses Bayesian and classical statistical methods for auditing. It has two major modules. The first relates to the test of transactions and the second relates to substantive tests of account balances. The first module uses a β distribution as a prior distribution and the second module uses a normal distribution. To provide conceptual support for BASS, there are two handouts available. The first is 'An Introduction to Probability As Related to Auditing Solutions'. The second is a paper entitled 'Decision Support and Expert Systems in Auditing: A Review and Research Directions' (see [28]).
Use requirements	The 'program' is a LOTUS template. IBM PC or PC Compatible, Lotus 2.01.

Contact	Mohammed J. Abdolmohammadi, Professor of Accounting, Department of Accountancy, College of Business, Bentley College, Waltham, Massachusetts 02154, USA. Tel. 617-891-2976.

Program	Bayesian audit sampling—variables
Synopsis	The software computes a risk level for a Bayesian variables sample, given prior probabilities and sample results (see [29]).
Use requirements	Only mainframe FORTRAN source code is available. Program would have to be compiled in an environment of choice.
Contact	Edward J. Blocher, Professor of Accounting, Accounting Faculty, School of Business, University of North Carolina, Chapel Hill, North Carolina 27599, USA. Tel. 919-962-3200.

Program	Variables sampling education support software (VSESS)
Synopsis	VSESS is a variables sampling program. It consists of three components. First, the SIM program and its companion, the REPORT program, are designed to permit the user to produce audit populations (details of accounts) of varying characteristics around which customized cases can be built. Second, the program SIZE accepts parameter estimates from users or permits editing by the user of previously saved parameters and calculates efficient samples for dollar-unit and for variables sampling methods.

Third, the program SAMPLE reads parameter files created by SIZE, accepts new parameter input or permits editing by the user of previously saved parameters and calculates efficient samples for dollar-unit and variables sampling methods. The user may choose to have a simulated population 'audited' by SAMPLE according to any of the five sampling methods for which parameters are available in a saved parameter file. SAMPLE provides upper and lower bounds (precision limits) of error for the account (population) and provides detailed sample statistics. Five cases are available with the software and documentation.

Use requirements	IBM PC or PC Compatible; 256K RAM; Two double-sided, double density disk drives.
Provider	Professors Urton L. Anderson and Robert G. May and Carolyn A. Miles
Contact	Professor Robert G. May, KPMG Peat Marwick Professor of Accounting, Department of Accounting, College of Business Administration, The University of Texas at Austin, Austin, Texas 78712-1172, USA. Tel. 512-471-5215.

Program	The computer-assisted data analysis (CADA) monitor
Synopsis	Written in BASIC, CADA is a multipurpose interactive package designed for non-specialist use. It provides computer-assisted instruction in data analysis and a variety of Bayesian statistical methods. It contains 422 programs, 204 000 lines of code, requiring six

megabyte of hard disk to store. Cost $600 (see Novick and Jackson[30]).

Use requirements   DEC VAX, PDP/11 RSTS and RT11, Prime BASIC and BASIC V, HP2000 and 3000.

Contact   The CADA Group Inc., 306 Mullin Avenue, Iowa City, Iowa 52246, USA.

megabyte of hard disk storage (cost $600
(see Novak and Jackson)

DEC VAX, PDP11 RSTS, and RSTE, Prime
BASIC and BASIC V, RB2000 and 8000

The CADA Group, Inc, 306 Mullin Avenue,
Iowa City, Iowa 52240 USA

Bibliography

Abdolmohammadi, M.J. Bayesian inference in substantive testing: An ease of use criterion. *Advances in Accounting*, **2**, (1985), 275–289.

Abdolmohammadi, M.J. Bayesian inference research in auditing: Some methodological suggestions. *Contemporary Accounting Research*, **2** (Fall 1985), 76–94.

Abdolmohammadi, M.J. Efficiency of the Bayesian approach in compliance testing: Some empirical evidence. *Auditing: A Journal of Practice and Theory*, **5**(2) (Spring 1986), 1–16.

Akresh, A.P., Loebbecke, J.L. and Scott, W.R. Audit approaches and techniques. In Abdel-Khalik, A.R. and Solomon, I. (eds) *Research Opportunities in Auditing: The Second Decade* (Sarasota, Florida: American Accounting Association, 1988).

Anderson, D. and Teitlebaum, A. Dollar unit sampling. *Canadian Chartered Accountant*, **102**(4), (1973), 30–39.

Ashton, R.H. Integrating research and teaching in auditing: Fifteen cases on judgement and decision making. *The Accounting Review*, (Jan 1984), 78–97.

Bailey, A.D. *Statistical Auditing: Review, Concepts and Problems*, (Orlando: Harcourt Brace Jovanovich, 1981).

Baker, H.K. and Haslem, J.A. Information needs of individual investors. *Journal of Accountancy*, (November 1973), 64–69.

Ball, R. and Brown, P. An empirical evaluation of accounting income numbers. *Journal of Accounting Research*, (Autumn 1968), 159–178.

Belkaoui, A. *Accounting Theory* (Orlando: Harcourt Brace Jovanovich, 1985).

Bertschinger, P. Switzerland National Paper, pp 93–97, *Proceedings of 4th Jerusalem Conference on Accountancy, Audit Risks and the Increasing Burden of Unlimited Liability*, (Institute of Chartered Accountants in Israel, 1986).

Blocher, E. and Robertson, J.C. Bayesian sampling procedures for auditors: Computer assisted instruction. *The Accounting Review*, (April 1976), 359–363.

Blocher, E. Assessment of prior distributions: The effect on required sample size in Bayesian audit sampling. *Accounting and Business Research*, **12**(45) (Winter 1981), 11–20.

Burgstahler, D. and Jiambalvo, J. Sample Error Characteristics and Projection of Error to Audit Populations. *The Accounting Review*, (April 1986), 233–248.

Chow, C.W. The Demand for external auditing: Size, debt and ownership influences. *The Accounting Review*, (April 1982), 272–291.

Churchman, Ackoff, Arnoff *Introduction to Operations Research*, (J. Wiley & Son, 1957), p. 210 et seq.

Crosby, M.A. Bayesian statistics in auditing: a comparison of probability elicitation techniques. *The Accounting Review*, (April 1981), 355–365.

De Finetti, B. Foresight: Its logical laws, its subjective sources. Reprinted in translation in H.E. Kyburg and H.E. Smokler (eds) *Studies in Subjective Probability* (Wiley, 1964).

Demski, J.S. *Information Analysis*, (Addison-Wesley, 1980).

Dworin, L. and Grimlund, R.A. Dollar unit sampling for accounts receivable and inventory. *The Accounting Review*, (April 1984), 218–241.

Dworin, L. and Grimlund, R.A. Dollar unit sampling: A comparison of quasi Bayesian and moment bounds. *The Accounting Review*, (January 1986), 36–57.

Fanning, D. How slow are the auditors in Britain? *Accountancy*, (August 1978), 44–48.

Felix, W.L. Evidence on alternative means of assessing prior probability distributions for audit decision making. *The Accounting Review*, (October 1976), 800–807.

Felix, W.L. and Grimlund, R.A. A sampling model for audit tests of composite accounts. *Journal of Accounting Research*, (Spring 1977), 23–41.

Felix, W.L., Grimlund, R.A., Koster, F.J. and Roussey, R.S. Arthur Andersen's new monetary unit sampling approach. *Auditing: A Journal of Practice and Theory*, **9**(3) (Fall 1990), 1–16.

Fienberg, S.E., Neter, J. and Leitch, R.A. Estimating the total overstatement error in accounting populations: *Journal of the American Statistical Association* (June 1977), 295–302.

Fischhoff, B., Hohenemser, C., Kasperson, R. and Kates, R. Handling hazards, pp 161–179. In J. Dowie and P. Leferere (eds) *Risk and Chance* (Milton Keynes: The Open University Press, 1980).

Foster, G. Quarterly accounting data: Time series properties and predictive-ability results. *The Accounting Review*, (Jan 1977), 1–21.

Garstka, S.J. and Ohlson, P.A. Ratio estimation in accounting populations with probabilities of sample section proportional to size of book values. *Journal of Accounting Research*, (Autumn 1979), 179–192.

Gray, I. and Manson, S. *The Audit Process: Principles, Practice and Cases*. (Van Nostrand Reinhold, 1989).

Grimlund, R.A. and Schroeder, M.S. On the current use of the Stringer method of MUS: Some new directions. *Auditing: A Journal of Practice and Theory*, **8**(1), (Fall 1988), 53–62.

Gwilliam, D. and Macve, R. The view from the top on today's auditing revolution. *Accountancy*, (November 1982), 116–121.

Gwilliam, D. *A Survey of Auditing Research*, (London: Prentice-Hall International, 1987).

Ham, J., Losell, D. and Smieliauskas, W. An empirical study of error characteristics in accounting populations. *Accounting Review*, (July 1985), 387–406.

Hamburg, M. *Statistical Analysis for Decision Making*, 3rd edn. (Harcourt Brace Jovanovich, 1983).

Haskins, M.E. and Williams, D.D. The association between client factors and audit fees: A comparison by country and by firm. *Accounting and Business Research*, **18**(70), (Spring 1988), 183–190.

Hey, J.D. *Data in Doubt: An Introduction to Bayesian Statistical Inference for Economists*. (London: Basil Blackwell, 1983).

Hylas, R.E. and Ashton, R.H. Audit detection of financial statement errors. *Accounting Review*, (October 1982), 751–765.

Johnson, J.R., Leitch, R.A. and Neter, J. Characteristics of errors in accounts receivable and inventory audits. *Accounting Review*, (April 1981), 270–293.

Kaplan, R.S. Statistical sampling in auditing with auxiliary information estimators. *Journal of Accounting Research*, (Autumn 1973), 238–258.

Kinney, W.R. A note on compounding probabilities in auditing. *Auditing: A Journal of Practice and Theory*, (Spring 1983), 13–22.

Kraft, K.H. Statistical sampling for auditors: A new look. *The Journal of Accounting*, (August 1968), 49–56.

Kreutzfeldt, R.W. and Wallace, W.A. Error characteristics in audit populations: Their profile and relationship to environmental factors. *Auditing: A Journal of Practice and Theory*, (Fall 1986), 20–43.

Lee, T.A. *Company Auditing: Concepts and Practices*, (London: Gee & Co., 1972).

Lee, T.A. The modern audit function: A study of radical change. pp 87–106. In Carsberg, B. and Hope, T. (eds) *Current Issues in Accounting*, London (Philip Allan: 1977).

Lindgren, B.W. *Statistical Theory*. (New York: The MacMillan Company, 1968).

Leitch, R.A., Neter, J., Plante, R. and Sinha, P. Modified multinomial bounds for larger numbers of errors in audits. *The Accounting Review*, (April 1982), 384–400.

Leslie, D.A., Teitlebaum, A. and Anderson, D. *Dollar Unit Sampling—A Practical Guide for Auditors*, (Belmont CA: Fearon-Pitman Publishers, 1979).

McRae, T.W. *Statistical Sampling for Audit and Control*. (New York: John Wiley & Sons, 1974).

McRae, T.W. *A Study of the Application of Statistical Sampling to External Auditing*. (London: Institute of Chartered Accountants in England and Wales, 1982).

McCray, J.H. A quasi-Bayesian audit risk model for dollar unit sampling. *The Accounting Review*, (January 1984), 35–51.

Menzefricke, M. and Smieliauskas, W. A simulation study of the performance of parametric dollar unit sampling statistical procedures. *Journal of Accounting Research*, (Autumn 1984), 588–604.

Moore, P.G. and Thomas, H. Measuring Uncertainty. *Omega*, Vol III, (1975), 657–672.

Moore, P.G. *The Business of Risk*, (Cambridge University Press, 1983), p. 50 et seq.

Neter, J. and Loebbecke, J.K. *Behaviour of Major Statistical Estimators in Sampling Accounting Populations—An Empirical Study.* Auditing Research Monograph No. 2, (USA: AICPA, 1975).

Novick, M.R. and Jackson, P.H. *Statistical Methods for Educational and Psychological Research,* (McGraw-Hill, 1974).

Otway, H.J. and Pahner, P.D. Risk assessment. *Futures,* **8**(2), (April 1976).

Plante, R., Neter, J. and Leitch, R.A. Comparative performance of multinomial, cell and Stringer bounds. *Auditing: A Journal of Practice and Theory,* (Fall 1985), 40–56.

Pratt, J.W., Raiffa, H. and Schaifer, R. *Introduction to Statistical Decision Theory,* (New York: McGraw-Hill, 1965).

Raiffa, H. and Schlaifer, R. *Applied Statistical Decision Theory,* (Cambridge, MA: MIT Press, 1961).

Ramage, J.G., Krieger, A.M. and Spero, L.L. An empirical study of error characteristics in audit populations, with discussion. *Journal of Accounting Research,* (Supplement 1979), 72–113.

Reneau, J.H. CAV bounds in dollar unit sampling: Some simulation results. *The Accounting Review,* (July 1978), 669–680.

Samuelson, P.A. Proof that properly anticipated prices fluctuate randomly. *Industrial Management Review,* **6,** (Spring 1965), 41–49.

Schultz, J.J. and Gustavson, S.G. Actuaries' perceptions of variables affecting the independent auditor's legal liability. *Accounting Review,* (July 1978), 626–641.

Shafer, G. and Srivastava, R. The Bayesian and belief-function formalisms: A general perspective for auditing. *Auditing: A Journal of Practice and Theory,* **9** (Supp. 1990), 110–137.

Solomon, I., Tomassini, L.A., Romney, M.B. and Krogstad, J.L. Probability elicitation in auditing: Additional evidence on the equivalent prior sample. *Advances in Accounting,* **1** (1984), 267–290.

Spelzler, C.S. and Stael von Holstein, C.A.S. Probability encoding in decision analysis. *Management Science,* **22**(3), (November 1975), 341–358.

Stamp, E. and Marley, C. *Accounting Principles and the City Code: The Case for Reform,* (Butterworth, 1970) pp 168–169, cited in T.A. Lee The modern audit function: A study of radical change. In Carsberg, B. and Hope, T. (eds) *Current Issues in Accounting.* (London: Philip Allan, 1977).

Stamp, E. and Moonitz, M. *International Auditing Standards,* (London: Prentice-Hall, 1979).

Steele, A. Another look at the levels of assurance issue in auditing. *Accounting and Business Research* **14**(54) (Spring 1984), 147–156.

Steinbart, P.J. Materiality: A case study using expert systems. *The Accounting Review,* (January 1987), 97–116.

St Pierre, K. and Anderson, J.A. An analysis of factors associated with lawsuits against public accountants. *Accounting Review,* (April 1984), 242–263.

Stringer, K.W. Practical aspects of statistical sampling in auditing. In

Proceedings of The Business and Economic Statistics Section, 1963, (Washington DC, American Statistical Association, 1963), pp 405–411.

Tamura, H. Analysis of the Garstka–Ohlson bounds. *Auditing: Journal of Practice and Theory,* 4(2) (Spring 1985, 133–142).

Tsui, K.W., Matsumura, E.M. and Tsui, K.L. Multinomial-Dirichlet bounds for dollar-unit sampling in auditing. *The Accounting Review,* (January 1985), 79–96.

Wallace, W.A. *The Economic Role of the Audit in Free and Regulated Markets.* (New York: Touche Ross, 1980).

Waters, R. The race is on to replace a rare commodity. *Financial Times,* (May 11, 1989), p. 13.

Watson, W.A., Philipson, T. and Oates, P.J. *Numerical Analysis: The Mathematics of Computing,* 2nd Edition, (Edward Arnold, 1981).

Watts, R.L. and Zimmerman, J.L. *Positive Accounting Theory,* (USA: Prentice-Hall International, 1986).

Weinstein, E.A. International commentator. *Proceedings of 4th Jerusalem Conference on Accountancy, Audit Risks and the Increasing Burden of Unlimited Liability,* (Institute of Certified Public Accountants in Israel, 1986).

Winkler, R.L. *Introduction to Bayesian Inference and Decision,* (Holt, Rinehart Winston, 1972).

Woolf, E. *Legal Liability and Practicing Accountants,* (London: Butterworths, 1985).

Author Index

Numbers in parenthesis relate to notes.

Subject Index